Problem Regions of Europe

General Editor: **D. I. Scargill**

North East England

Kenneth Warren

OXFORD UNIVERSITY PRESS

Oxford University Press, Ely House, London W. 1

Glasgow New York Toronto Melbourne Wellington
Cape Town Ibadan Nairobi Dar es Salaam Lusaka Addis Ababa
Delhi Bombay Calcutta Madras Karachi Lahore Dacca
Kuala Lumpur Singapore Hong Kong Tokyo

© Oxford University Press 1973

First published 1973
Reprinted 1974

Filmset by BAS Printers Limited, Wallop, Hampshire
and printed in Great Britain
at the University Press, Oxford
by Vivian Ridler, Printer to the University

Editor's Preface

Great economic and social changes have taken place in Europe in recent years. The agricultural labour force has almost everywhere contracted, in some places very rapidly, and the lack of alternative forms of employment in rural areas has resulted in large-scale movements of farmers and farm labourers in search of work in the cities. The scale of this drift from the land can be gauged from the fact that in the six (original) Common Market countries the agricultural work force was halved between 1950 and 1970: from approximately 20 millions to 10 millions. In many areas this rural exodus has made it possible to carry out much needed reorganization of farm holdings, but it has also brought with it problems concerning, for example, the provision of services to a contracting population and the need to establish new forms of land use where farming is no longer profitable.

Contraction of the labour force has also taken place in several old-established industries. These include coal-mining, shipbuilding, and the more traditional textile industries, where the effects of a shrinking market have been made more severe by automation, which has substituted machines for men. The coal-mining industry of Western Europe shed something like two-thirds of its labour force during the 1950s and 1960s. Wherever a large proportion of the working population was dependent upon a declining industry of this kind, the problems of adjustment have been severe. Many schemes have been devised to attract alternative forms of employment but, despite incentives, it has often proved difficult to attract new firms because of the old industrial areas' legacy of dirt, derelict landscape, poor housing, and, in some places, bad labour relations.

Problems of a different kind have arisen as a result of the continued growth of large cities such as London and Paris, or of groups of closely related cities as in the case of Randstad Holland. The reasons for such growth are several. To the manufacturer the big city offers the advantage of a local market, a varied labour force, and easy access to suppliers and other manufacturers with whom he needs to maintain close links. To them and even more to the service industries a city location offers a prestige location, and the enormous expansion of service activity, especially office-work, has contributed greatly to postwar urban growth. Attempts to control the increase of employment within cities have had some success as far as manufacturing industry is concerned but very little with regard to office work.

Problems resulting from city growth include traffic congestion, high land prices, pollution, and social stress brought about by factors such as housing shortages and travelling long distances to work. Yet the city continues to attract migrants for whom the image is still one of streets paved with gold, whilst the established resident is loath to leave the 'bright lights', the football club, or the familiar shops.

Geographers, in the past, have been reluctant to focus their attention on regional problems. The problem was thought to be a temporary phenomenon and therefore less worthy of consideration than regional characteristics of a more enduring nature—the landscape or the chimerical *personality* of the region. Yet such is the magnitude, persistence, and areal extent of problems of the kind referred to above that the geographer would seem to be well justified in approaching his regional study by seeking to identify, measure, and even seek solutions to problems.

'Devenant alors un cadre de recherche, la région sera choisie en fonction de certains problèmes et des moyens qui permettent de les aborder avec profit' (H. Baulig). Indeed it has been suggested that regions can be defined in terms of the problems with which they are confronted.

Additional stimulus for studying regional problems arises from the interest which politicians and planners have recently shown in the region as a framework for tackling such issues as the relief of unemployment, the siting of new investment, and the reorganization of administrative boundaries. Governments have long been aware of the problems resulting from economic and social changes and various attempts have been made to solve them. Development Areas and New Towns in Great Britain, for example, represent an attempt to deal with the problems, on the one hand, of the declining industrial areas and, on the other, of the overgrown cities. Such solutions can hardly be described as regional, however. Other countries have recognized the problems of their over-populated rural areas and the Cassa per il

Mezzogiorno, the Fund for the South, was set up by the Italian government in 1950 in order to encourage investment in the South. The E.E.C. has also channelled funds via its Investment Bank, both to southern Italy and to other parts of the Common Market distant from the main centres of economic activity. Planning of this kind shows an awareness of the regional extent of economic and social problems, though in practice much of the actual work of planning was undertaken on a piecemeal, local, and short-term basis.

Since about 1960, however, the continuing nature of the problems has persuaded most European governments to adopt longer-term and more comprehensive planning measures, and the importance of seeking regional solutions has been increasingly stressed. The last ten years have, in fact, witnessed the setting up of regional planning authorities in many European countries and to them has been given the task of identifying regional problems and of finding solutions to them. A large number of reports have been published following research carried out by these authorities, and individual governments have introduced regional considerations to national planning. The French *métropoles d'équilibre,* for example, were devised in order to introduce new vigour to the regions via the largest provincial towns.

One of the drawbacks to regional planning of this kind is the outdated nature of local government boundaries, most planning decisions having to be implemented through a system of local government more suited to nineteenth than to late twentieth century conditions. Some experts have thus advocated a regional alternative to existing local government areas, and it is interesting to note that the Royal Commission on Local Government in England (the Maud Report), whilst not supporting so radical a change, nevertheless introduced the idea of *provinces* within which broad planning policies could be carried out. Supporters of the regional idea argue that a growing trend toward State centralization is bringing about a reaction in the form of renewed popular interest in regions, their history, industrial archaeology, customs, dialect, and so on.

The revival of interest in regions, both for their own sake and as a practical aid to planning or administration, makes particularly timely the appearance of a series of geographical studies concerned with *Problem Regions of Europe.* The present volume is one of 12 studies comprising such a series.

The twelve regions have been selected in order to illustrate, between them, a variety of problems. The most obvious of these are: problems of a harsh environment, of isolation, of industrial decay, of urban congestion, and of proximity to a sensitive political frontier. One or other of these major problems forms the dominant theme in each of the volumes of the series, but they have not been studied in isolation. Where it has been thought relevant to do so, authors have drawn attention to similar problems encountered in other parts of the continent so that readers may compare both the causes of problems and the methods employed to solve them. At the same time it is recognized that every region has a number of problems that are unique to itself and these peculiarly local problems have been distinguished from those of a more general kind.

Although the precise treatment of each subject will vary according to the nature of the region concerned and, to some extent, the outlook of a particular author, readers will find much in common in the arrangement of contents in each volume. In each of them the nature of the problem or problems which characterize the region is first stated by the author; next the circumstances that have given rise to the problems are explained; after this the methods that have been employed to overcome the problems are subjected to critical examination and evaluation. Each study includes indications of likely future developments.

All the authors of the series have considerable first-hand knowledge of the regions about which they have written. Yet none of them would claim to have a complete set of answers to any particular regional problem. For this reason, as well as from a desire to make the series challenging, each volume contains suggestions for further lines of inquiry that the reader may pursue. The series was conceived initially as one that would be helpful to sixth-form geographers but it is believed that individual volumes will also provide a useful introduction to the detailed work undertaken by more advanced students both of geography and of European studies in general.

D.I.S.

St. Edmund Hall
August 1972

Contents

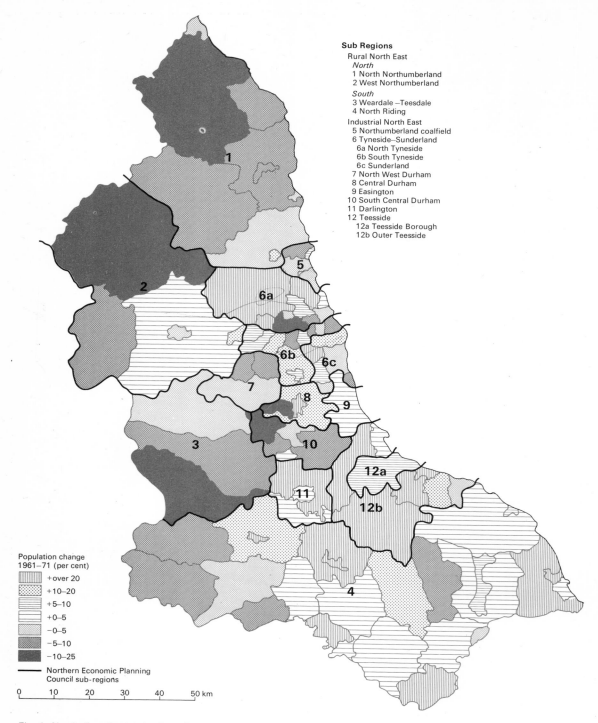

Sub Regions

Rural North East
North
1 North Northumberland
2 West Northumberland

South
3 Weardale –Teesdale
4 North Riding

Industrial North East
5 Northumberland coalfield
6 Tyneside–Sunderland
  6a North Tyneside
  6b South Tyneside
  6c Sunderland
7 North West Durham
8 Central Durham
9 Easington
10 South Central Durham
11 Darlington
12 Teesside
  12a Teesside Borough
  12b Outer Teesside

Population change
1961–71 (per cent)

+over 20
+10–20
+5–10
+0–5
–0–5
–5–10
–10–25

—— Northern Economic Planning
Council sub-regions

0   10   20   30   40   50 km

Fig. 1. North-East England sub-regions and population change, 1961–71

North-East England has problems in common with other parts of Europe. Problems of a contracting coalmining industry are shared with regions such as the Ruhr and the northern coalfield of France. The need to replace traditional heavy industries with new growth ones is also encountered in other industrial regions. But the North-East is far from being an exclusively industrial area and the problems of the rural fringe have more in common with those of, for example, the Highlands of Scotland or the Massif Central. Some problems must, of course, be unique to a particular region, not least those which result directly from its location, and many commentators have sought to draw conclusions from the position of the North-East in relation to the more prosperous South-East of England or to the major cities of the Common Market. The scale and overall combination of problems must also be unique to a particular area and the paragraphs which follow provide a pointer to the nature of this general problem status of the North-East.

Population change and migration

The problems of the under-developed world make modern commentators much less ready than many in the past to seize on population growth as an index of a prosperous, happy nation. However, within a developed nation, regional population trends may well provide an index of economic well-being: a boom area growing rapidly, a problem region lagging behind. Since the early years of the industrial revolution the population of the North-East as a whole has followed an uneven course—slower growth than that of the nation to the mid-nineteenth century, three-quarters of a century of more rapid expansion after that, and then again slower growth. At the 1801 census the North-East had about 5·3 per cent of the population of England and Wales, 5·1 per cent in 1851, 6·7 per cent in 1901 and 7·1 per cent in 1921. By 1971 its share had fallen to 6·0 per cent. It is perhaps particularly disturbing that between 1961 and 1971, while national help to the North-East regional economy was greatly increased, population decline was rapid—from 6·26 per cent of that of England and Wales in 1961 to 6·02 per cent in 1971.

Population change is the product of the balance between natural increase and net migration, itself the resultant perhaps of very large emigration from or immigration to a region. Generally, and ignoring for the present non-economic considerations such as social welfare or amenity, continuing net immigration is an indication of general economic well-being while net emigration points to regional problems. Migration is quality-selective affecting particularly the younger adults and therefore the regional birth-rate. It is also, though this is more difficult to indicate statistically, skill- and enterprise-selective; there is in fact an inter-regional as well as an international brain drain.

In its period of most rapid expansion the North-East grew not only by high rates of natural increase but by large-scale immigration. However, by 1965 it was reckoned that 81·8 per cent of the persons living in the Northern Region (including the small populations of Cumberland and Westmorland as well as that of the North-East) had been born there, as compared with as few as 46·4 per cent in the Eastern Region. Throughout the last half-century the North-East has been an area of net outmovement. In the 1960s the average annual number was 6000 though it fell towards the end of the decade.

These changes in population are in large part the after-effect of the passing of an age when economic growth was led by a narrow range of heavy industries in which the North-East shared prominence along with other major coalfields. Since then there has been a continuous struggle to adjust to a changing national economic structure—a process made difficult both by industrial inheritance and location within Britain.

Employment and wage levels

The North-East—and the Northern Region, of which it is by far the largest part—has lagged behind the nation in the growth of its workforce. Between 1959 and 1970 the workforce in Great Britain grew by 0·53 million or +2·4 per cent. In the Northern Region there was a decline of 18 000 or −2·3 per cent. Consideration of the Standard Industrial Classification (S.I.C.) shows that, although the Northern Region's economic structure is shifting to a closer approximation to the national pattern, it still has too high a representation in the decline or slow-growth categories and is poorly represented in the rapidly expanding or

TABLE I
Economic Structure 1959 and 1970. Great Britain, Northern Region, Midlands, and South-East

S.I.C. Order		Great Britain 1959	Great Britain 1970	London and South-East 1959	London and South-East 1970	East and West Midlands 1959	East and West Midlands 1970	Northern Region 1959	Northern Region 1970
				Percentage of all employees					
I.	Agriculture, Forestry & Fishing	2·99	1·65	1·34	1·16	3·27	1·54	2·81	1·51
II.	Mining & Quarrying	3·83	1·85	0·27	0·20	5·43	3·01	13·04	5·07
III.	Food, Drink & Tobacco	3·64	3·84	3·35	2·95	3·39	3·42	2·67	3·25
IV.	Chemicals & Allied Industries	2·38	2·39	2·28	2·34	1·37	1·29	4·49	4·70
V.	Metal Manufacturing	2·66	2·63	0·60	0·65	5·29	5·23	4·39	4·41
VI.	Engineering & Electrical Goods	8·82	10·05	10·02	10·43	10·79	11·89	7·70	10·44
VII.	Shipbuilding & Marine Engineering	1·28	0·84	0·42	0·54	0·09	0·07	4·95	3·05
VIII.	Vehicles	3·96	3·72	2·54	3·04	7·64	7·38	1·27	1·07
IX.	Metal Goods not otherwise specified	2·34	2·83	1·67	2·02	5·84	6·63	0·89	1·18
X, XI, XII.	Textiles, Leather, Leather Goods, Fur, Clothing & Footwear	6·72	5·32	3·43	2·20	7·44	6·73	3·82	4·81
XIII, XIV.	Bricks, Pottery, Glass, Cement, Timber, Furniture, etc.	2·80	2·80	2·69	2·51	4·11	3·84	2·16	2·67
XV.	Paper, Printing & Publishing	2·62	2·89	4·12	4·05	1·47	1·66	1·09	1·49
XVI.	*Other Manufacturing*	*1·29*	*1·56*	*1·58*	*1·64*	*1·38*	*2·03*	*0·77*	*1·04*
	All Manufacturing	*38·57*	*38·95*	*32·78*	*32·44*	*48·86*	*50·47*	*34·27*	*38·21*
XVII.	Construction	6·55	5·90	6·44	5·34	5·86	5·15	6·91	7·19
XVIII.	Gas, Electricity & Water	1·72	1·70	1·87	1·71	1·57	1·63	1·50	1·67
XIX.	Transport & Communications	7·55	6·99	8·88	8·61	5·29	4·74	7·18	5·77
XX.	Distributive Trades	12·53	11·83	14·35	12·97	10·32	9·83	11·64	11·55
XXI.	Insurance, Banking & Finance	2·42	4·25	4·97	7·41	1·23	2·30	1·28	2·07
XXII.	Professional & Scientific	8·81	12·57	9·26	13·07	7·45	10·80	7·61	12·42
XXIII.	Miscellaneous Services	9·16	8·07	12·86	9·41	6·17	5·99	7·91	8·07
XXIV.	Public Administration & Defence	5·77	6·20	6·91	7·62	4·62	4·49	5·75	6·37
	Total (thousands)	21,870	22,404	5,493	7,698	3,645	3,651	1,298	1,270

Note: London and the South-East has undergone major boundary changes.

growth industries; decline in its old staple industries has not been fully made good by increase in other manufacturing lines and in the more rapidly growing non-manufacturing categories. (Table 1.)

In the 1960s the North-East is estimated to have lost 155 700 jobs by closure of plant, rationalization of work and so on, and to have received 159 700 new ones. This apparently successful, if perilously close balance has been upset by population growth of 3·1 per cent.

Partly because of the region's industrial structure, partly because of the shortfall of jobs in relation to numbers of workers, partly, no doubt, as a result of a wide range of other factors including tradition and reputation, wages are still below the national level. Between 1960 and 1970 average weekly earnings for male manual workers increased by 92 per cent in the United Kingdom and 94 per cent in the Northern Region, but in October 1970 the rate in the Northern Region was still only 97 per cent of the national average, as against 104 per cent for the South-East and 105 per cent in the West Midlands. It is true that the rate in the South-West Region was only 93 per cent of the national average and in East Anglia 92 per cent, but in both of these areas agricultural employment is much more significant.

Unemployment

Largely because of the continuing contraction of the old staple trades, unemployment—the most obvious and certainly the most commonly adopted index of problem status—is at higher levels in the North-East than in the nation, and at any time the ratio of vacancies to unemployed workers is lower. Indeed in nine of the twenty-five post-war years to the end of 1970, the average annual unemployment rate in the North-East has been at least twice the national average. The worst run of years was in the early 1960s when the rate was double the national rate for five consecutive years. Major investment in the Development Areas reduced the disparity after that, but although £260 million of government money was invested in the North-East between 1966 and 1970, the average for those years was still 4·24 per cent as compared with 2·26 per cent nationally. By August 1971, as new conditions and policies rapidly increased the numbers of the unemployed, the national rate was 3·7 per cent and that in the North-East 7·4 per cent.

Socio-economic expressions of deprivation

House and car make up the two largest investments of the average family. North-East car-

ownership rates are below the national average; housing values are below those in any other region of Britain. By the second quarter of 1971 the average price of all existing houses mortgaged in Britain was £5509, but in the North-East only £4086: for new houses the comparative figures were £5544 and £4560.[1] Northern school buildings are older and fewer children stay on at school after they reach the minimum leaving age than in favoured areas.

In some areas pollution is a severe threat to the environment and to the population, and some 20 000 acres of the Northern Region is derelict land, within the terms of the official definition— 'land so damaged by industrial or other development that it is incapable of beneficial use without treatment . . .'. This is a greater acreage than in any other planning region, and most of it is within the North-East.

These various indices establish the undoubted problem character of the North-East. The popular image, the view held by the man-in-the-street, has invested this status with a host of associations, most of them drab, some of them half-truths, others woeful caricatures, but all of them detrimental to a balanced assessment. Half-remembered personal impressions from a speedy journey through the region and television or film presentations of old industrial landscapes—dirty, perhaps semi-derelict, and apparently filled with grimy and frequently embittered and aggressive workers, and with very few inhabitants from other socio-economic groups—give at best an unbalanced view of the region. At worst they confirm the Andy Capp image of '. . . a community that baths in zinc tubs in front of coal fires and thinks of little else than beer, bingo, and wifebaiting'.[2] In fact, as well as pit villages, shipbuilding, steel, or chemical towns, the North-East contains major and in some cases dynamic urban areas; there is also a very lively regional culture, by no means all of it of the working-class image which is retailed as North-Eastern in the rest of Britain. Furthermore the whole of the mineral-working and industrialized area is surrounded by a broad rural fringe containing some of the finest, least spoiled landscapes in Britain.

REFERENCES
1. Nationwide Building Society quoted by the North-East Development Council.
2. *The Times*, 10 December 1971.

2 The Historical Background to Present Problems

Before the industrial revolution the North-East represented both a peripheral and a relatively poor part of the English economy. Difficulty of land access to the core area of the State was a persistent problem. The power of the Prince Bishops of Durham, the exploits of the Percy family, the romantic, if brutal feuds, and Scottish incursions into Redesdale were all indicative of the march-land status of the North-East. As late as the eighteenth century people from the Hartlepool area used to speak of a journey further south than Northallerton as 'going into England'. The distribution of wealth as indicated by hearth or poll tax returns, and density of population in so far as it can be gauged before the 1801 census, both suggest an ill-favoured region.

In the later Middle Ages and early modern period, growth of coastwise traffic in coal to London lessened the effect of remoteness for the small area around the estuary of the Tyne and to some extent round the lower Wear, and contributed especially to the wealth and pre-eminence of the city of Newcastle upon Tyne. In the eighteenth century, a growing demand, new pumping machinery, and the development of tramways widened the radius of economic coal-working, but even so the developed area remained a zone near to the two estuaries. By the 1820s the Tyne was already a heavily industrialized river based on settlements extending from well above Newcastle to the sea, and Newcastle itself had already become a regional capital of more than usual significance.

At this time, with spiralling demand—from London and East and South coast ports, from foreign markets around the North Sea, from local industry, and soon from railways within the region and the additional industries which they encouraged—the developed area of the coalfield was rapidly extended; it spread outwards from the old estuarine areas as wagonways and then railways opened new sections: the interior of North-west and South-west Durham, the coal beneath the Magnesian Limestone of the east Durham plateau, then, late in the nineteenth century, the Ashington section of the Northumberland field, and, shortly after 1900, the last area to be developed along the Durham coast near to and south of Easington. The haphazard pattern of economic growth which followed this process was summed up well by a correspondent of the *Mining Journal* in March 1841: 'Few changes have been more rapid than the physical aspect of south Durham—once the scene of rural quiet and agricultural pursuits. The face of the country is now studded with large collieries, each of which has its own colony of houses surrounding it, where every article of food and clothing may be obtained, and every resource found within its own confines.'[1] As this comment suggested, the settlement pattern of County Durham in particular was transformed. The number of settlements more than doubled in the nineteenth century, and it is significant that over half the parishes in the diocese of Durham in the 1930s had been created since 1850.[2] It could not be realized then that immense problems were being laid up for the mid-twentieth-century planner. The growth of the railway network resulted in the emergence of Darlington as an economic growth point. It had been a notable market town and had already added manufacture of linens and worsteds. Now its railway junction location led to its selection as a centre for the manufacture of railway equipment and this in turn encouraged the location there of metal and metal fabricating trades.

In spite of its richness in coal, and its great new railway developments, the North-East was relatively unimportant in iron production until after the mid-nineteenth century. In 1852 the share of its three counties was only 5·4 per cent of the United Kingdom total for pig iron as compared with 30·2 per cent for Staffordshire, 28·7 per cent for Scotland, and 25·8 per cent for Wales and Monmouthshire. The low yield and high costs of its Coal Measure iron ores were the main reasons for this backwardness. The opening of the Cleveland Main Seam on the hillsides south of Eston in 1850, however, unloosed yet another genie of growth, one whose activities in less than half a century transformed the Teesside flats, from Stockton to Redcar and at Hartlepool, from good pastureland for race- and work-horses into a major industrial area. Here all the emphasis was on metal—as Lady Bell declared at the beginning of the twentieth century, Middlesbrough was '. . . a place in which every sense is violently assailed all day long by some manifestation of the making of iron'. The growth of this district's output justified new railways which penetrated the hill country to the south, and scattered the harsh and formerly sparsely populated Cleveland parishes with boom ironstone mining villages. Iron and, later, steel manufacture was of some importance on Tyneside into the 1920s but competition from Teesside gradually killed off the works on the coalfield with the exception of Consett in high North-west Durham.

The requirements of the coastal trade in coal, the vessels for which were small and subject to a very high mortality rate during winter storms, encouraged a proliferation of yards building in wood, especially on the two main coal estuaries. With the advance of iron shipbuilding in mid-century the North-East added a favourable supply situation for the chief raw material to the demand conditions which had initially encouraged the industry. Blyth, Hartlepool, and the Tees became important shipbuilding centres, but in most years the Wear and Tyne retained their lead.

In heavy chemicals there was a wholesale change of location within the North-East over the half-century to 1930. One hundred years ago Tyneside shared with the Mersey basin an importance in alkali manufacture and its ancillary activities, notably production of sulphuric acid, which made them the leading heavy chemical districts of the world. For various reasons, mainly connected with technical and material supply changes, the Tyneside trade shrank rapidly after the 1870s, and in the mid-1920s I.C.I. closed the last plants. By this time Billingham was a rapidly growing pointer to the future stature of Teesside in a new range of heavy chemicals.

Other basic trades of the North-East were heavy engineering—locomotive and rolling-stock building, constructional engineering, production of industrial equipment—and an electrical engineering trade, developed in the last years of the nineteenth century and strongly localized on Tyneside.

Coal, steel, shipbuilding, chemicals, and engineering made up a formidable and interrelated growth sector. On the other hand the end products of all the basic trades were strongly biased in the direction of producers' goods for marketing outside the region and to a large extent outside Britain. There were periods of acute and sometimes of prolonged depression, as in the mid- and late-1870s and the middle years of the 1880s, but, these apart, economic advance was rapid. Between 1841 and 1881 the population of England and Wales increased by 63·3 per cent, that of the North-East by 112·0 per cent. A new surge of expansion in the early years of the century, followed by the First World War, maintained boom conditions through to 1920 and kept the old industrial areas in the forefront of the national economy. The population of England and Wales grew by 16·5 per cent between 1901 and 1921, that of the North-East by 23·5 per cent. These figures suggest that, although it remained an area of more than average growth, its momentum for expansion was already decreasing; the changes in the industrial structure of Britain and its competitive position within the trading world were moving against the North-East, even though the symptoms that were soon to make recognition of the region's malaise unavoidable had not yet broken the surface.

In the 1920s overseas coal outlets were lost, sometimes for political reasons, as with the U.S.S.R., sometimes because of new or more effectively organized competition, as from Poland or the Ruhr, sometimes because of a switch to alternative energy supplies, as with the progress in hydro-electric installations in Scandinavia. Coal outlets within the region also shrank, in part because of the chronic 1920s depression in steel. Shipbuilding, over-expanded with inferior equipment in the war, languished in an over-supplied market and in its turn dragged the steel industry still further down. Following the great expansion in electricity generation, electrical engineering was booming, and the new Teesside chemical trade expanded spectacularly, but these were still too small a factor in the regional and even the sub-regional economy to relieve the general depression. There was distress, and calls for protection and for rationalization were made in various old trades, but no shadow of a co-ordinated policy for an individual industry appeared and even less one for the regional economy as a whole. Between 1921 and 1931 the population grew by 5·7 per cent in England and Wales; in the North-East it grew by 1·1 per cent. The region had entered the phase of visible decline.

After the Great Depression of the early 1930s, reconstruction of some of the basic trades was begun, and the first, very tentative steps were taken towards a Development Area policy. Revival at this time was mainly connected with the rearmament drive. Because of the War there was no 1941 Census, but the Registrar General's 1939 mid-year estimates provided a guide to the effects of the 1930s. Over the eight years since the 1931 Census, the population of England and Wales had grown by only 3·9 per cent but the North-East showed a net decline of −4·3 per

Dennis Wompra

Tow Law, County Durham, one of the larger stranded communities on the western edge of the Durham coalfield. Established as an ironworks centre in the 1840s it is now desperately struggling to adapt to the changing economic circumstances. It is helped by its location on the A68

cent or 115 000. The pattern of decline, like the previous pattern of growth, was differentiated within the North-East—Durham with its great dependence on coal feeling the effect especially severely.

Following World War II, the firm application of Development Area policies for four years, and then general economic expansion until 1957–8, helped to continue the wartime prosperity in all the old basic sectors of the regional economy; also some important new growth industries were introduced. Although the average annual unemployment rate for the North-East was only once over 3·0 per cent in the ten years after 1948, the average for the period was 2·42 per cent as compared with 1·51 per cent for Great Britain. The 1961 Census registered a 15·4 per cent

increase over 1931 for the population of England and Wales, but only 6·6 per cent for this region. From boom area the North-East had become decisively, and apparently permanently, a problem region. Students of the region, and still more those planning its future, are faced with the critical difficulty of determining to what extent its problems are the result of a peculiar economic structure, the outcome of its unbalanced economic growth, and to what extent they are inherent, the intrinsic problems of a region peripheral to the national economy.

REFERENCES
1. *Mining Journal*, 13 March 1841.
2. G. TURNER, *The North Country* (Eyre and Spottiswoode, London, 1967), p. 305.

The North-East is a region the various parts of which have widely differing economic structures and trends (Fig. 1, p. 6). Almost all the region falls within the urban spheres of influence of the three main retailing foci: Tyneside–Wearside, Darlington, and Teesside. These commercial nuclei are set within an economic core area characterized by the impact of man on the natural landscape in the conduct of mining or manufacture, and extending for some 90 km along the coast from Amble to south of Redcar and stretching westwards to a line running slightly west of Darlington, Bishop Auckland, and Consett, crossing the Tyne west of Blaydon and from there via Morpeth back to Amble. This area contains the bulk of the region's wealth, population, and problems.

The core is surrounded by high country: in the south the Jurassic mass of the North York Moors and the Cleveland Hills, to the west the high Pennine moorland, and northwards a series of lower hill ranges and then the great dome of the Cheviots. Access to the core area from the rest of England and from Scotland is limited to two lowland routes—the broad Vale of York, and the coastal lowland of Northumberland, narrowing to the old strong-point of Berwick-on-Tweed at the Border. The valley of the South Tyne and the Irthing give a higher, but still good through route to Carlisle. All other important routeways into the region are more difficult: via Stainmore, from Penrith via Alston to Hexham, along the Yorkshire coast from Scarborough, and from Tweedale and Teviotdale over Carter Bar and through Redesdale. Each route passes through the rural fringe, an area the landscape, economy, and society of which seem a world away from those of the core, but a problem sub-region nevertheless.

The rural fringe

The outlying districts of the North-East are characterized by rural problems frequently accentuated by height above sea-level, severity of climate, and remoteness from regional markets and services. Parallels with regions such as the French Massif Central have already been noted. In the northern part population has declined; in the southern part decline has been followed by new growth as commuting distances from the Teesside industrial area or the West Riding conurbation have increased (Table 2).

Naturally employment structures are very different from those of both region and nation (Table 3). As populations have declined and daily travel to work in neighbouring conurbations has increased, so the rural fringe has secured a disproportionately small amount of new employment. In the fifteen and a half years to mid-1971, rural Northumberland was awarded Industrial Development Certificates expected to yield a total of only 5609 jobs (3693 male)—3·7 per cent and 3·6 per cent respectively of the North-East total for an area still having 4·7 per cent of the region's population.* Moreover much of this new employ-

* Realized levels of new employment fall short of those anticipated when I.D.C.s are granted.

TABLE 2
Population of counties of the North-East and of selected Rural Districts, 1951, 1961, 1971 (thousands)

	1951	1961	1971
Durham and North Riding:	1976·9	2066·7	2132·5
Rural Fringe districts of Durham and North Riding:			
Barnard Castle R.D.	18·7	17·0	15·9
Weardale R.D.	9·3	8·4	8·0
Leyburn R.D.	6·4	6·2	5·9
Hemsley R.D.	4·5	4·3	4·8
Aysgarth R.D.	3·6	3·3	3·0
Northumberland:	798·4	821·2	794·8
Rural Fringe districts of Northumberland:			
Belford R.D.	5·1	5·0	4·6
Glendale R.D.	7·6	7·0	6·1
Bellingham R.D.	5·3	5·3	4·6

TABLE 3
Employment structures June 1967 by major categories

S.I.C. Orders	Great Britain	Percentage of total North-East	Rural North-East (South)	Rural North-East (North)
Order I Agriculture etc.	1·9	1·6	9·0	13·1
Order II Mining and Quarrying	2·4	8·5	1·1	7·4
Orders III–XVI All Manufacturing	38·0	37·5	15·6	13·5
Orders XVII–XXIV All Services	57·5	52·0	73·9	65·6

Source : North-East Development Council.

ment was in areas peripheral to the true rural fringe, as for instance in Prudhoe (which could more realistically be regarded as an outlying part of the Tyneside conurbation) or in market towns such as Alnwick, Hexham, Morpeth. Much the largest part of the rural fringe has been left without new jobs to counterbalance the contraction in agricultural employment.

The combination of growth by natural increase with net out-migration has given the rural population an unbalanced age structure, with a disproportionately large share of older persons. At the end of the 1960s 25·7 per cent of males in the 'Industrial North-East north', and 28·0 per cent in the 'Industrial North-East south' were under 14 years of age; 9·4 per cent and 8·6 per cent were 65 or over. In the 'Rural North-East north' and 'south' the proportions under 14 were 24·5 and 23·7 per cent, and over 65, 10·8 and 11·4 per cent.

Naturally the economic and social status and prospects of various parts of the rural fringe vary according to their population structure, physical conditions, and proximity to industrial and urbanized areas (Table 4 and Fig. 1). There have been variations between districts, but overall the good arable and grass country at the northern end of the Vale of York has retained its population helped by overflow from Teesside and Darlington and by the growth of the North Riding county town of Northallerton. In the Cleveland Hills, decline threatened by changes in the rural economy and closure of the last of the ironstone mines has also been checked by urban influences. Whitby has held its own as a small port, has hopes of new activity from potash development, and is a most attractive holiday centre—but in winter it has high unemployment. Whitby's impact on Cleveland has been negligible as compared with

that stemming from the population explosion from Teesside. In the five Cleveland districts of Stokesley, Guisborough, Loftus, Saltburn and Marske, Skelton and Brotton, population rose by 16 000 or 27·3 per cent between 1961 and 1971, as compared with only 5·7 per cent in the Teesside County Borough.

The Yorkshire dales show more positive signs of decay, except in Richmond and Bedale Rural Districts, both affected by service establishments, in the case of the former by the big Catterick camp. The four Rural Districts to the west and south-west of these lost 1800 persons between 1951 and 1971: a fall of 6·9 per cent in the first ten years and 5·9 per cent in the second. Startforth R.D. in the North Riding, and Barnard Castle and Weardale R.D., which cover the whole of Durham west of the coalfield, have been combined in the sub-regional planning of the Northern Region. Apart from Barnard Castle, a market-town of 5000, they are rural, with limestone-working, a little mining of fluorspar and the relics of their once extensive and now dead lead-mining industry. Their 1971 population was only 82·4 per cent that of 1951, though again the decline was rather slower in the 1960s than the 1950s.

In Northumberland, the very large Hexham Rural District has slightly increased its population as a result of overspill from Tyneside and from the market town of Hexham, with its close on 10 000 inhabitants. Twelve miles to the north of the Tyneside conurbation, and nearer to populous colliery districts, Morpeth has grown and acts as an important shopping focus. Northwards, there has been a general decline. In the seven Rural Districts north and west of Hexham and Morpeth R.D.s the decline between 1951 and 1971 varied from 7·6 to 22·0 per cent but for all of them the

TABLE 4
Natural population change and net migration in the rural North-East since 1951

	1951–6		1956–61		1961–6		1966–9	
	Natural Change	Net Migration	Natural Change	Net Migration	Natural Change	Net Migration	Natural Change	Net Migration
North Northumberland	1901	− 1826	2208	− 1690	1838	− 708	581	− 90
West Northumberland	453	− 808	552	+ 16	536	+ 404	18	+ 332
Weardale/Teesdale	181	− 613	440	−1,928	331	− 571	78	− 208
Rural North Riding	3311	− 353	3672	− 652	5435	+ 10 145	2855	+ 5987

Note: The figures are for Northern Economic Planning Council sub-regions, which in some cases include growth areas near to conurbations.

decline totalled 6333. Alnwick and Berwick, much more remote from great centres of population than Morpeth or Hexham, together declined in population by 5·8 per cent or over 1100 between 1951 and 1971.

Economic structure and land-use conflicts

Most of the North-East rural fringe is hill country the reputation of which has been based on the quality of its sheep bred for sale to the lowlands. Hill-farming faces a host of problems, basically environmental. The area is sparsely populated and remote from urban services and amenities. Climate is harsh, soil poor, and drainage bad, which means that highly desirable improvements cannot be justified by better returns. It is, for instance, economically impossible to justify tile drainage costing £50 to £60 an acre on hill land worth only £30 an acre, so the hill-farmer must make do with open ditches. Application of fertilizer would greatly improve grass and carrying capacity. However improvements might cost £20 an acre and the typical small hill-farmer lacks the capital for this sort of improvement. In 1969 the North Pennines Rural Development Board was established under the terms of the Agricultural Act to consider the 'special problems and special needs of rural areas of hills and uplands'. It was designed to help farmers with better buildings, to encourage larger and therefore more viable farm units, and to improve rural communications. However, its other terms of reference (in a brief life ending in its abolition early in 1971) included the search for a co-ordinated policy for the uplands, involving reconciliation of conflicting land-uses. The uplands are no longer the undisputed province of the hill-farmer and his flocks.

Almost one hundred years ago Hugh Miller spoke of the remarkable landscape contrast between the uplands and the eastern lowland parts of Northumberland where '. . . we exchange the moors for enclosed ground, dry-stone walls for hedgerows, rare sprinklings of birch for a sufficiently varied wooding . . .'.[1] Even fifty years ago the uplands of the North-East were fine open moorland with heather and bog and areas of fell and crag. Since then forests have been established over large areas, both by the Forestry Commission and private interests, and forest acreage is still increasing. The Forestry Commission is restricted to land of negligible agricultural value so that the present controversy about forestry applies in large measure to private afforestation.

Investment in forestry is high—a 1967 estimate was £80 per acre as compared with about £5 in existing hill farms—but government money for the Forestry Commission and planting grants and tax concessions for the private concern make development attractive. Moreover by 1970 timber prices had risen, whereas hill-farming paid no more than ten years before. In the 1950s an economic comparison made at the Agricultural Economics Research Institute of Oxford, showed that in England and Scotland (though not in Wales with its milder climate) forestry gave better returns on the uplands than sheep, and price trends since then have widened the gap.[2] The more enterprising sheep farmer, or the pioneer of better methods, will dispute this, but there are social as well as private gains from trees rather than sheep. It has been estimated that sheep-farming employs one man for every 1000 acres but forestry gives direct employment to one man for every 100 acres and, as well as helping to maintain existing villages, has created the essentially new forest villages such as Kielder and Byreness in Northumberland.

The old strategic argument for forestry carries little weight in an age of nuclear weapons, and the economic case must take into account E.F.T.A. and wider groupings involving association with countries which can grow timber more cheaply. Nevertheless, although home-grown timber as yet provides barely 10 per cent of the national needs, this represents a saving of £70m foreign exchange annually. In addition the forests frequently occupy ground otherwise economically useless. In the early days of afforestation pasture-lands were frequently blocked out by injudicious plantation layout, but this problem is much less serious now and there are compensations for the sheep-farmers, notably protection from the wind. The Forestry Commission has been accused of spoiling the landscape by planting solid stands of sombre conifers, but occasional roadside fringes of deciduous trees have generally mollified the opposition. Afforestation can, however, still be an emotive issue, as in 1970 when the Rural Development Board gave a private group permission to plant 600 acres of conifers in Langstrothdale beyond upper Wharfedale.

Water supply for the core area is another controversial matter in the rural fringe. Early in the century the Catcleugh reservoir was built to supply Tyneside. Recently the attempts to satisfy the thirst of heavily industrialized Teesside have aroused a much more amenity-conscious generation. In the mid-1960s threats of heavy Teesside unemployment were used to ensure that parliamentary powers were given for the building of Cow Green reservoir in an area which not only possesses magnificent wild limestone-scar scenery but also contained an association of Pleistocene flora unique in Britain. A few years later an attempt to develop a reservoir in an area of quieter beauties, Farndale in Cleveland, was frustrated. Attention then turned to a project of an unprecedented size and remoteness. The Northumbrian River Authority announced a £27 million project, involving a 2800-acre reservoir extending nine miles up the North Tyne valley from Falstone to Kielder. Some 200 persons would need to be rehoused and the Northumberland County Council would have to realign roads in the North Tyne valley. At first sight the scheme appears rational and likely to provide little disturbance, but the implications are in fact very great, for 'an area where there are more trees and grouse than humans could become a major centre for water-sports and for tourism'.[3] Already by 1971 some were speaking of the amenity possibilities of 'Kielder Water'. Undoubtedly this will change the whole quiet beauty of the area,

Fig. 2. Upper Redesdale, 1921–2

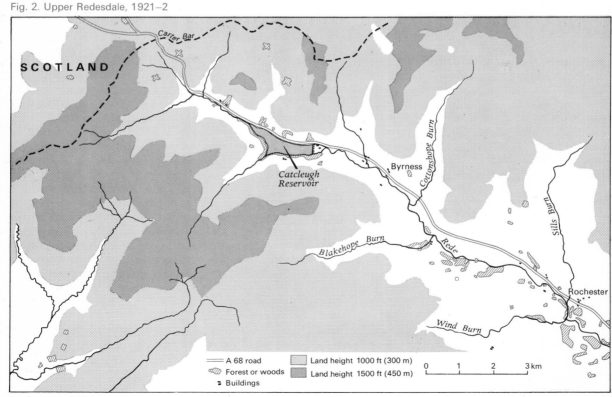

and by autumn 1971, before the decisive public inquiry, there were 120 objectors to the scheme, including most local interests. The River Authority has argued that the alternative would be six smaller schemes which would thereby spread any unfavourable landscape impact. The opposition maintains that a less offensive development on the Irthing could provide all the water needed until the mid-1980s.[4]

The land-use conflicts of sheep-farming, forestry, and water supply are made keener by the spread of recreation and tourism and in some cases military activity in the rural fringe (Figs. 2 and 3). The inter-war controversy over the acceptability of forests was keen but limited to an elite: now the multitudes are involved. It is now recognized that some middle course must be found between the preservation of the countryside and unrestricted access to increasingly mobile and affluent townsmen. The Forestry Commission has reacted positively with National Forest Parks and by co-operating in amenity development; in Northumberland, for instance, by providing Nature Trails. Elsewhere in the North-East other pressures threaten both the traditional countryside and amenity: the search for minerals in west Durham, encouraged by fresh, liberal incentives from the government in 1971; Fylingdales early

warning station; oil and gas exploration; and potash development in the Cleveland Hills.

In this region the tourist is as yet inadequately provided for in terms of hotel or restaurant accommodation, as he who tries to find dinner or bed in August will soon discover. Under the terms of the Development of Tourism Act 1969, government funds are available to cover 20 per cent of the cost of new hotels and extensions to existing ones in the United Kingdom as a whole and 25 per cent in Development Areas, so long as the work was begun before April 1971 and is completed by early 1973. Northumberland and Durham have 69 projects under this scheme, representing a total investment of £7.3 million. In other respects too, tourism in the region is belatedly moving ahead. Foreign visitors to Hadrian's Wall are being encouraged and the Northumberland County Council and the National Coal Board are developing a 190-acre 'super-recreational centre' at Druridge Bay. In many respects such developments are desirable, but the preservation of the unique quality of the rural North-East will not be easy, and the quiet unspoiled beauty of sand, dune, and wide sweeping bay at Druridge will be only a memory. The major consolation of the amenity interest in the North-East must be that the rural fringe is wide

Fig. 3. Upper Redesdale, 1961–2

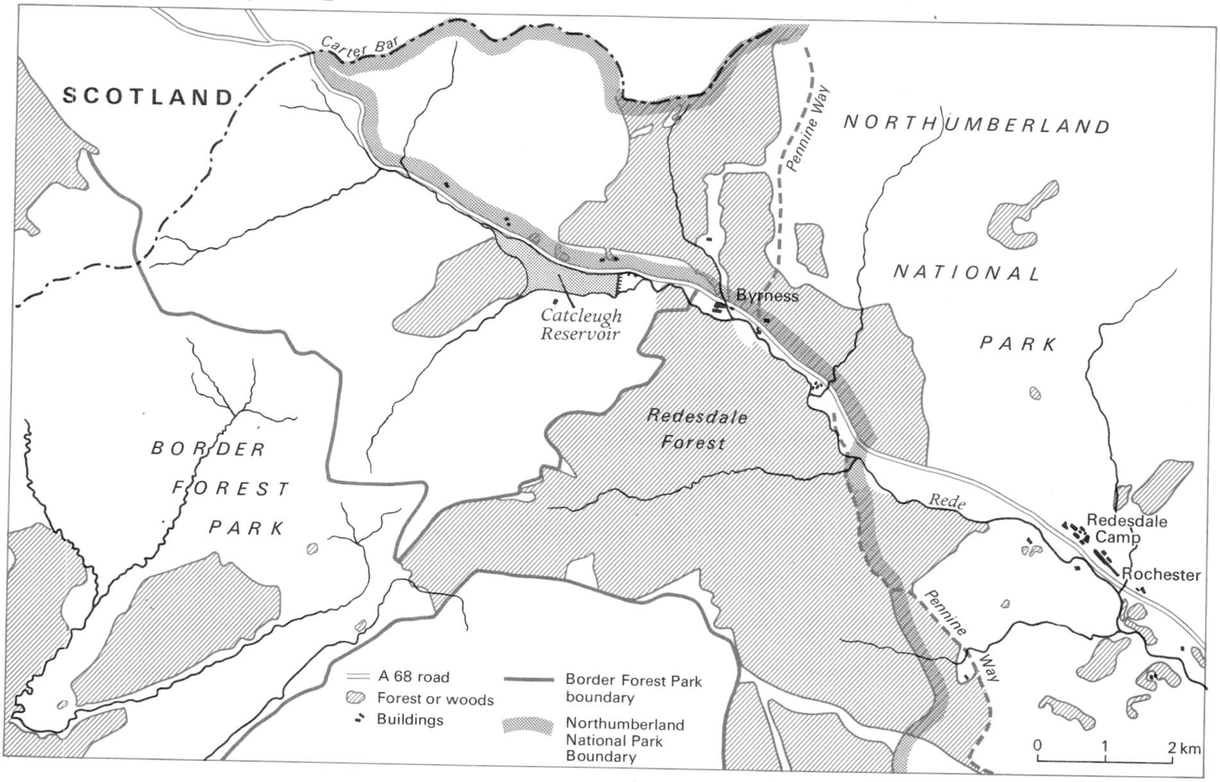

17

Turners (Photography) Ltd

The North Tyne valley below the site of the proposed Kielder reservoir. The small community on the right is Falstone

enough to concede such sites on its border while still preserving the wastelands for those who prefer them. As pressures mount, the need for careful allocation of land-use categories will greatly increase.

The fringe areas of the North-East have become a kind of supply region for the industrial/ urbanized districts that house over 85 per cent of the region's population: a source of workers to a small extent, a place of homes for people working in the towns, and an area for recreation and the provision of water. In the future these demands will grow. Within the rural fringe, retailing and other urban functions will become still more concentrated in the bigger units.

REFERENCES
1. H. MILLER, 'Northumberland', *Encyclopaedia Britannica*, 7th edn. (1884).
2. C. CLARK, letter to *The Times*, 11 March 1965.
3. The *Guardian*, 2 August 1971.
4. *Newcastle Journal* passim.

4 Problems in their Sub-regional Context: II. The Coalfield

The rural fringe contains only 106 000 out of the 1 125 000 workers in the North-East. The rest are inhabitants of the smaller area made up of the coalfield, the Darlington district, and Teesside (Table 5).

The observant traveller on the A68 from Darlington to Corbridge will recognize that he roughly follows a line of division between two regions. Westwards lie the wide uplands and the fine broad dales of rural Durham; eastwards the ground falls away to an area in which are settlements, smoke, and all the signs of population and activity. The pattern of lights at night brings out the contrast even more clearly. The road in fact roughly delimits the western edge of the Durham coalfield. Further east the A1 is another convenient, if arbitrary line of division: between landlocked and coastal district mines; between generally smaller, shallower, and older pits and the deeper pits and bigger settlements to the east; between an area of problems with few redeeming advantages and one which, though troubled by problems enough, has also compensating advantages—milder climate, newer settlements, better communications, and proximity to bigger foci of population.

North-west Durham

The North-west Durham sub-region lies north of a line from Tow Law to Durham and east of the Derwent (Fig. 4). For sub-regional planning purposes it is made up of the Urban Districts of Consett and Stanley and the Lanchester Rural District, though the latter extends beyond the coalfield. Much of it is high hill-country deeply dissected by the streams running into the Wear or directly down to the Tyne. Although it contains important valley settlements such as Shotley Bridge, Hamsterley, and Rowlands Gill, the biggest communities are hill-top ones and associated with mining. The centre of Annfield Plain is between 230 and 250 metres above sea level and the bleak square at the centre of Consett is at over 260 metres. A hill location for these major settlements and many smaller ones provided the opportunity of sinking shafts through the whole of the productive coal series but has rendered access difficult.

In the nineteenth century the excellent coking coals of this area were opened up and a great surge in economic growth occurred. In 1871 Stanley was characterized as '. . . a hamlet in the north of Durham, four and a half miles N.N.E. of Lanchester'.[1] By 1901 it had 13 500 people. As late as 1960 there were thirty pits within a five-mile radius of the town, but by mid-1970 all but nine had closed and in only two of the remainder had there been no fall in employment. In the whole of the North-west Durham sub-region, 9300 men worked in mining and quarrying in 1964 but within four years this had fallen to 5400. In 1964 only one other industrial category employed over 750 persons. This was metal manufacture with 6037 workers, almost

TABLE 5
Economic structures in the industrial North-East, 1967

Sub-region	Percentage of total employment		
	Mining and Quarrying	Manufactures	Services
Northumberland Coalfield	41·8	17·2	39·9
Easington	50·5	13·1	34·5
South-central Durham	14·9	42·7	40·7
North-west Durham	17·6	36·1	44·3
Central Durham	12·0	17·3	69·3
Tyneside/Wearside	7·8	38·8	52·3
Teesside	0·9	49·8	48·2
Darlington	0·3	47·4	50·0

Note: In 1967 the proportion of employees in manufacturing industry was 38·0% in the United Kingdom and 37·5% in the North-East.
Source: N.E.D.C. 1969.

all of them at Consett. Whereas Stanley has lost population throughout the post-war period, accelerating in the 1960s, Consett held its population fairly well in the 1950s—the works even took on some 600 redundant miners in the early 1960s—and even though rationalization has since then been accompanied by population decline in the town, the rate of shrinkage has been smaller than at Stanley. The prospect of much more radical change at Consett (p. 34), threatens to remove the sheet anchor of the troubled North-west Durham economy.

Lanchester R.D., after a sharp drop in the 1950s, held its population better in the 1960s. It had fewer collieries in the immediate vicinity, and retained two of these located in the Browney Valley. Moreover it is on lower ground, nearer the Great North Road than Consett or Annfield Plain, and well placed for access to Durham via a road improved in the 1930s. However, it has had scant success with its industrial estates, and the 1966 Sample Census showed a daily net migration to Stanley Rural District where, at Stanley and Annfield Plain, Ever Ready and Ransome and Marles respectively have built important new plants.

In 1964 North-west Durham had 3·2 per cent of all insured employees in the North-East. Contraction in its basic trades has been greater than in most parts of the region so that, not surprisingly, it has received a more than proportionate share of planned industrial employment. In the 14 years to the end of 1969 Industrial Development Certificates (I.D.C.s) were secured which were expected to generate jobs amounting to 4·2 per cent of those anticipated for I.D.C. permissions in the North-East as a whole. Some of the region's industrial estates have been especially successful in attracting firms employing men.

South-west Durham

Between the Browney and the Wear stretches the remnant of the once-famous coking coal district of South-west Durham. On the riches of this area Crook grew to pre-eminence among nineteenth-century British coke districts. There were eight pits in this district in 1960 and as late as 1964 mining and quarrying provided 8600 jobs or 20 per cent of the total in Bishop Auckland, Shildon, Crook, and Spennymoor Urban Districts. By 1970 all eight pits had closed. Ten other pits south or south-west of Bishop Auckland and extending to the southern limit of the coalfield also closed in the 1960s. As in North-west Durham, the National Coal Board was able to soften

the impact of pit closure by transferring men to surviving pits, and subsidizing their longer journey to work. In the early 1960s one coach carried men daily from the Bishop Auckland area to Sunderland, a round trip of some forty-five miles.

Population has declined and the decline here has been still greater than in North-west Durham—a fall of 12·1 per cent between 1951 and 1971 in Bishop Auckland, Crook and Willington, Spennymoor, and Tow Law districts as opposed to 11·2 per cent in the North-west sub-region. However as pit closure began earlier in the South-west sub-region, industrial diversification has also proceeded further. Additionally the eastern fringes of the sub-region are extremely well favoured from the point of view of communications. Aycliffe industrial estate is only six miles from Bishop Auckland; and Spennymoor, just west of the A1, has become another growth focus. Meadowfield estate at Brandon was opened in 1968 and has similar locational advantages and Dragonville estate, east of Durham, is also

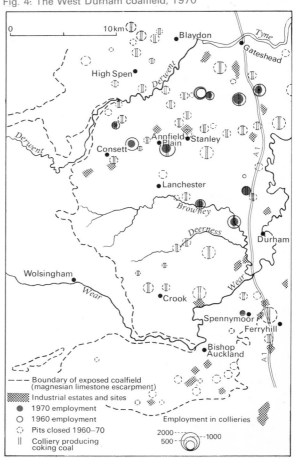

Fig. 4: The West Durham coalfield, 1970

--- Boundary of exposed coalfield (magnesian limestone escarpment)
▒ Industrial estates and sites
● 1970 employment
○ 1960 employment
◌ Pits closed 1960–70
‖ Colliery producing coking coal

Employment in collieries

2000
500 — 1000

accessible. The smaller estates in the coalfield towns away from the A1 have been noticeably less successful, particularly in building up male employment. Although workers travel from a distance to the favoured estates there is already a significant population change differential favouring the eastern section of the sub-region. Between 1961 and 1971 population decline in Bishop Auckland U.D. was 8·5 per cent, in Spennymoor only 0·2 per cent, but in generally more remote Crook the fall was 14·7 per cent, and in the case of Tow Law 12·8 per cent.

Central Durham

The Central Durham sub-region is a planner's hybrid with diverse economic characteristics and trends. In the eastern part of the Browney and Dearness valleys it includes part of the West Durham coalfield, while on the other hand it takes in Durham Municipal Borough and Durham Rural District. Population has declined in the coalfield section and there has been growth in the rest of the sub-region, especially in the 1960s. The

Fig. 5. The East Durham coalfield, 1970

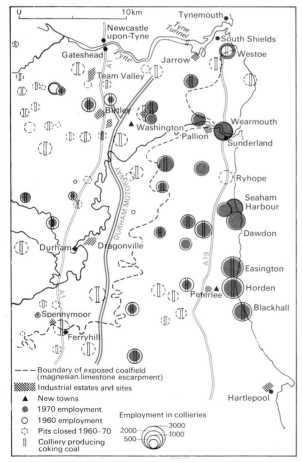

— — — Boundary of exposed coalfield (magnesian limestone escarpment)
▨ Industrial estates and sites
▲ New towns
● 1970 employment
○ 1960 employment
◌ Pits closed 1960–70
‖ Colliery producing coking coal

Employment in collieries
2000····⎯3000
500··⎯1000

inclusion of Durham City helps to give a much more 'normal' economic structure than in most of the coalfield.

Easington
The south-eastern part of the Durham coalfield has been called the Easington sub-region (Fig. 5). Throughout the post-war years until the late 1960s population grew here, though towards the end of this period the rate of increase fell away. The economy is extraordinarily unbalanced, dependence on coal being very high. In the 1960s a few small- to medium-sized pits in the Trimdon and Wingate areas closed, but the big central units in Easington, Horden, and Blackhall have held their workforce well. Manufacturing and services employment are of little account; in 1967 no single S.I.C. manufacturing order employed even as many as 3 per cent of the number of males in mining and quarrying.

Foundations have been laid for a new manufacturing and urban focus following the designation of Peterlee New Town in 1948. Its growth has been plagued by a series of troubles: mining subsidence in the early days, a reluctance of mine families to move from old pit communities —an account of the late 1950s spoke of the '... hopeless gulf of incomprehension between planners and planned'[2]—and problems of attracting industry to an area rather poorly connected to the national road network. At a time when mining in Easington sub-region was buoyant it was acceptable that most of the slow growth of employment in the Peterlee industrial estate should be for women, but in the late 1960s and early 1970s, when redundancy of pit workers increased, there were still remarkably few outlets for men. Even though the area is perhaps intrinsically better placed than either North-west or South-west Durham, unemployment rates have risen to comparable levels.

North-east Durham
Colliery closure has caused some severe local problems in the North-east Durham sub-region. These difficulties (examined in two notable case-studies) involve, as far as the individual is concerned, retraining, finding re-employment for the older man, social adjustments to new places and types of work (and often a decrease in earnings), and, for the planner, the difficulty of knowing when is the right time to provide new factories—if built too soon they will be short of men until the pit closes, and if too late, unemployment will be high and men will move away.[3] Adjustment has been eased by proximity to both the Wearside and

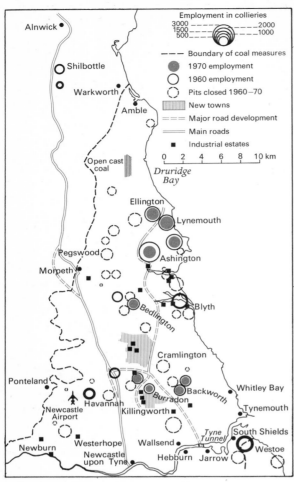

Fig. 6. The Northumberland coalfield, 1970

still, from Blyth through Ashington to the big pits at the southern end of Druridge Bay.

Until the end of the 1950s this was a growth area: coal output in the Ashington district increasing by one million tons and employment by 2000 jobs in the ten years after nationalization. At the beginning of 1961, eighteen collieries in the Ashington, Bedlington, and Newbiggin area produced five and a half million tons of coal and employed 14 540 men. Within seven years, output had fallen by almost one-fifth, the number of pits was cut to ten, and employment fell by 4800. By the middle of 1970 there were six pits employing 6235 men. Decline was especially severe in Bedlingtonshire, where the 1967 output was just over 40 per cent that of 1957 and employment had fallen by two-thirds.[4]

In the Northumberland coalfield sub-region in 1967 mining and quarrying employed 56·5 per cent of the male working population and the only two important manufacturing categories together employed just 5·6 per cent of the males. Closure of the Blyth shipyard in 1966 caused a major loss of jobs at the same time as coalmining employment contracted rapidly, and altogether in two years to June 1968 the sub-region lost a total of some 300 jobs in manufacturing and 2300 in extractive industry. Service employment remained unchanged, and construction registered an increase of some 200. By June 1969 the unemployment rates were 8·0 per cent and 10·2 per cent (for males), the highest figures for any North-East sub-region.

Most new industrial estates in this sub-region have grown only slowly, but in the late 1960s the rate of job creation was stepped up impressively. Cramlington new town, a Northumberland County Council project to provide both for overspill from Tyneside and a new urban focus for an ill-serviced section of the coalfield, had played an important role, but the most spectacular development has followed the 1968 decision to build an Alcan aluminium smelter at Lynemouth. This has provided construction jobs, permanent new metal working employment, a minor boost to the port of Blyth, and the guarantee of about 1000 jobs in Ellington and Lynemouth pits which will supply the Alcan power station.

REFERENCES
1. *The Imperial Gazeteer of England and Wales 2*, 1872.
2. The *Guardian*, 17 June 1959.
3. J. W. HOUSE and E. M. KNIGHT, *Pit Closure and the Community* (University of Newcastle upon Tyne 1967). *Ryhope : A Pit Closes* (H.M.S.O. 1970).
4. N.C.B. and Miss L. T. BRADFORD, *Coal-mining Towns —Transition or Decline?* Unpublished M.A. thesis, (University of Newcastle upon Tyne 1968).

Tyneside conurbations and to Washington New Town, designated in 1964 and planned to increase in population from 20 000 at that date to 80 000. Washington, with substantial locational advantages over Peterlee, including a long frontage on the Durham motorway, was primarily designed to accommodate conurbation overspill, but it also provides a new commercial focus and place of employment for the North-east Durham coalfield communities.

Northumberland

In the Northumberland coalfield (Fig. 6), mining along the Tyne below Newcastle ceased long ago and the pits on the northern and western edge of the conurbation closed in the 1960s. Mining remains important in Longbenton and Seaton Valley U.D.s. The present core is further north

5 Problems in their Sub-regional Context: III. The Industrial Estuaries and the Darlington Sub-region

Of the North-East's 2·93 million inhabitants 2·03 million live in four urban/industrial areas, together occupying only a small part of the region: Tyneside, Wearside, Teesside, and the Darlington area (Table 6). This 69·3 per cent of the region's population is the most favoured if judged by a number of economic criteria. Activity rates for men, and still more for women, are above the regional average. Unemployment levels have been lower than in the coalfield. Rateable values in the four urban sub-regions averaged £18 800 for every thousand persons in 1969 as compared with £17 900 and £17 200 in the Rural North and Rural South respectively and as little as £13 600 in the three major coalfield sub-regions of North-west and South-central Durham and Easington. Car-ownership rates are generally higher, though figures for household amenities and overcrowding are not uniformly so. Although population growth rates have generally been well above those for the region they lag well behind the national figure. In 1966 these four areas had 85·6 per cent of the region's manufacturing labour force and 73·5 per cent of its employment in service industries.

Since the decline of the coalfield economy began fifty years ago, more of the population and employment growth has been concentrated in these urban and industrial areas. Population growth rates alone suggest a clear distinction between the two southern, dynamic members, and Wearside and Tyneside as areas of slower economic growth. The distinction between them can be refined by ranking them according to a range of characteristics. These bring out the outstanding position of the Darlington sub-region. Teesside ranks next, and again the northern areas trail far behind with, on balance, South Tyneside and Wearside ranking lower than North Tyneside (Table 7).

Wearside

Wearside is the smallest and by many criteria the least favoured of the industrial sub-regions (Fig. 7a). It is true that between 1951 and 1971 Sunderland County Borough and its three neighbours to north and west, the U.D.s of Boldon, Washington, and Houghton-le-Spring, grew by 9·4 per cent whilst the population of the Tyneside conurbation shrank by 3·7 per cent, but in this period much of the growth generated by the Tyneside economy spread beyond the conurbation boundary to Seaton Valley, pre-eminently to Castle Ward, and, at the end of the period, to Washington.

Over one-quarter of Wearside male workers are employed in primary industry, overwhelmingly coalmining. Ryhope pit has closed. Closure of Silksworth pit, with a loss of over 600 jobs on the southern edge of the urban area was announced in early autumn 1971, but Wearmouth pit within the County Borough is likely to remain a major local employer.

Wearside has a narrow manufacturing range, with shipbuilding and marine engineering, and electrical engineering the two leading categories (Table 8). Although shipbuilding is a more important contributor to manufacturing employ-

TABLE 6

Population of major urban/industrial sub-regions of the North-East, 1951, 1961, 1971

Administrative sub-region*	1951 thousands	1961 thousands	1971 thousands	1951–71 percentage change
Darlington district	99 204	110 127	119 839	+ 20·8
Teesside	483 367	538 173	581 165	+ 20·2
Sunderland	316 636	333 096	337 848	+ 6·7
Tyneside	981 028	1 010 468	987 060	+ 3·0
Total	1 880 235	1 991 864	2 025 912	+ 7·8
North-East	2 784 448	2 888 029	2 927 541	+ 5·2
England and Wales	—	—	—	+ 11·0

*Planning Council sub-regions.

TABLE 7

Economic and social characteristics of the main urban/industrial areas of the North-East

Sub-Region or District	Population change 1961–9 %	Dwellings completed per 1000 population 1963–8	Households with more than 1·5 persons per room	Houses with exclusive use of 3 basic amenities 1966 % total	Industrial rateable value % change 1963–7	Rateable value per thousand people in £000s (i) Domestic	(ii) Shops	(iii) Offices and other commercial	(iv) Industrial	Activity Rate % 1966 Female	Male
North Tyneside	(0·4%)	(31·4)	1·8%	[73·7%]	(−3·1%)	[20·3]	4·4	[4·6]	5·3	40·1	(81·8)
South Tyneside	2·3%	45·1	1·7%	(67·5%)	3·1%	(16·1)	(2·3)	2·4	6·7	40·1	83·4
Wearside	1·8%	43·1	(2·1%)	71·5%	6·8%	17·5	3·8	(2·2)	(3·9)	38·2	83·0
Teesside	7·6%	[47·3]	1·2%	71·3%	5·4%	18·1	3·2	2·5	[16·0]	(37·4)	[85·3]
Darlington	[8·2%]	46·7	[0·6%]	72·4%	[22·1%]	[20·3]	[4·8]	3·4	10·2	[41·3]	83·8

[ ]   Highest rank   ( )   Lowest rank

Source: Northern Economic Planning Council, *Sub-Regional Statistics*.

Fig. 7. Industrial land-use on lower Tyneside and Wearside, 1971

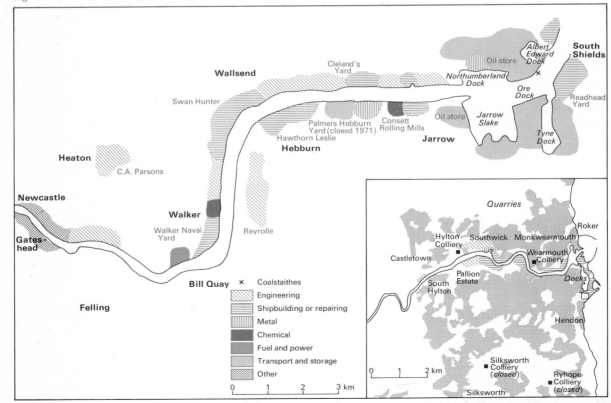

New employment from I.D.C.s 1965-9 as % total in manufacturing in 1968	Unemployment rate. Mean of June and December figures 1965-9	Cars per 1000 people 1966	Ranking no. of cases in which district ranks highest	no. of cases in which district ranks lowest
28·7%	(5·13%)	130	2½	4½
32·7%		(104)	—	4½
	4·78%	106	—	3
(19·0%)	3·52%	131	3	2
[46·1%]	[2·63%]	[152]	8½	—

ment than on Tyneside or Teesside, the Wear offers the least favourable environment for the industry in the region. The river is deeply incised, narrow, and meandering, so that there is little low, flat land near the river for efficient yard layout, and launching is by no means easy. Merger has cut the number of firms to two, and specialization on standardized dry cargo vessels has brought success in spite of inherent difficulties.

Engineering and electrical engineering are less important to the sub-regional economy than to that of Tyneside, and activity is concentrated on rather lighter lines, as indicated by the higher proportion of women—37·8 per cent of the total workers in this order on Wearside in 1967/8 as compared with 27·5 per cent in South Tyneside and 17·3 per cent in North Tyneside. The lighter electrical firms on Wearside are less tied to the investment cycle than the Tyne's heavy electrical giants, but sharp oscillations in economic prosperity in the late 1960s and early 1970s led to some failures among Sunderland firms.

Industrial estates in the Sunderland area have grown much more rapidly in the 1960s than those of the North-East as a whole. By 1970 their employment of 13 600 at Pallion, Southwick, and Hendon was over one-quarter of all Wearside manufacturing employment as compared with well under one-fifth in the case of Tyneside. There is little room for further growth at Pallion, and manufacturing expansion in Sunderland is imperilled by the fact that it is away from the main lines of movement in the North-East; in spite of its proximity it seems strangely remote from Newcastle. The services sector is small. Job creation has failed to keep pace with job losses, and out-migration and unemployment rates have been high. From 1961 to 1968 net out-migration from the Sunderland district was 3·6 per cent of the 1961 population as compared with 2·8 per cent on Tyneside. From 1965 to 1969 the average June unemployment rate on Tyneside was 3·5 per cent; on Wearside 4·4 per cent. In August 1971 the ratio of unemployed to unfilled vacancies was 11 to 1 for Tyneside but 28 to 1 for Wearside. Wearside has a stark grandeur but a more difficult physical setting and a harsher man-made environment than Tyneside. If one adds to this its less diverse economic structure, smaller size, and relative remoteness, one must conclude that it is likely to be a continuing problem sub-region.

Tyneside

Tyneside is the economic heart and head of the North-East (Fig. 7). Its population of just over one million is one-third of the regional total and

TABLE 8

Estuarine sub-regions : male employment by major industrial categories, 1968

	Thousands					Specialization: two chief manufacturing orders as % of total
	S.I.C. VII Shipbuilding and Marine Engineering	S.I.C. V Metals	S.I.C. IV Chemicals	S.I.C. VI Engineering and Electrical Engineering	All other Manufactures	
Wearside	9·2	1·6	1·7	9·2	10·4	61·1%
North Tyneside	16·1	2·2	5·6	19·1	21·5	54·6%
South Tyneside	8·1	2·5	4·3	27·6	15·3	61·7%
Teesside	5·1	31·9	28·1	15·7	17·9	60·8%
					Great Britain (1967)	40·1%

76 per cent greater than that of Teesside. It had 37·7 per cent of all employment in the North-East in 1968, 40·6 per cent of employees in manufacturing, and 39·5 per cent of service industry employment.

Its leading industrial order is the very wide category of engineering and electrical engineering, accounting for 9·5 per cent of all employment in North Tyneside and 21·6 per cent on South Tyneside in 1967. The two leading firms are heavy electrical equipment makers, Reyrolle at Hebburn and the associated firm of C. A. Parsons at Heaton. Electrical engineering has suffered severely, however, in the economic troubles of the late 1960s. In spring 1971 Reyrolle, employing 8000 manual workers, announced that as many as 900 would be paid off over the next few months. However the principal regional impact of the increased government spending on nationalized industries, announced late in 1971 to boost Development Area activity, will be on the Tyneside electrical engineering firms, in the form of orders for power station equipment.

Whereas electrical engineering is more important in employment terms on the south side, shipbuilding employs twice as many men on the north bank of the Tyne as on the south. Wallsend and Walker are the main centres of the Swan Hunter Group. On the south bank are smaller yards at Hebburn and South Shields. The main Tyne repair yards are at North Shields, Wallsend and Hebburn. Tyneside shipbuilding has made substantial losses, employment has fallen, and in an area where shipbuilding component and service work is so important the effects of bad trade are multiplied. Significantly, unemployment down-river has been highest. Between June and August 1971 the number unemployed in Newcastle rose by 27 per cent but in South Shields by 34 per cent, at Walker the rate almost doubled, and the increase in the Employment Exchange areas of Jarrow, Hebburn, and Wallsend was over 100 per cent.

Much new manufacturing employment has been attracted to Tyneside, North Tyneside alone receiving new firms or expansions which were expected to provide over 24 000 jobs between 1956 and the end of 1969 (available figures for South Tyneside inconveniently include Wearside, an extended district for which the total was 41 900). Much of the new employment has been located in estates peripheral to the old estuarine core. English Industrial Estate Corporation sites at West Chirton (North Shields), the Bede estate between Jarrow and South Shields, and another site at Jarrow increased their total work force from 9165 to 12 825 between 1960 and 1970. Over the same period employment at Team Valley towards the westward edge of the conurbation and its very small counterpart north of the river at Newburn, went up from 13 460 to 20 060. Killingworth, Cramlington, and other smaller sites exemplify the same trend away from the old riverine centres.

There have also been important shifts in the service industries. Tyneside, defined by the Northern Economic Planning Council, had 37·6 per cent of the North-East's professional service employment, 39·6 per cent of that in public administration, and 46·5 per cent of the financial service employees in 1967/8. A high proportion of tertiary sector activities are located in North Tyneside and especially in Newcastle upon Tyne itself.

With manufacturing employment down-river declining, new manufacturing foci emerging, and the growing importance of the tertiary sector, the economic and geographical structure of the sub-region is changing. Between 1961 and 1971 the conurbation population fell by 5·9 per cent. Together Gateshead, Hebburn, and South Shields declined by 8·1 per cent and the 6·2 per cent increase at Felling, partly due to the eastward movement of Gateshead people, was in total only 2200 as compared with Gateshead's loss of 8800. On the north bank, Wallsend's population fell by 4000 or 8·1 per cent, that of Tynemouth by only 3·5 per cent. Outlying districts at the seaward end such as Boldon and Whitley Bay, grew, but the landward side was the area of growth, at Ryton and Newburn, at Whickham (15·7 per cent), and in Castle Ward, where there was an outstanding growth of 12 000 or 50 per cent in the decade.

Outward spread of population and new foci of employment make the Tyneside journey-to-work complex. An additional feature is the significance of the Tyne as a barrier. There is no bridge below Newcastle, though ferries have long existed between Hebburn and Walker, Hebburn and Wallsend, and North and South Shields, and since 1967 the Tyne Tunnel (a toll tunnel) has provided a link between Jarrow and Howdon. Between Newcastle and Gateshead four road and pedestrian bridges provide a link which is effective enough except at peak hours, and further up river there are other bridges between Blaydon and Scotswood, and Ryton and Newburn. Though facing each other across the river, the communities below Newcastle have been effectively much farther apart. The journey-to-work survey of the 1966 Sample Census showed that

Jarrow, a community of net outward daily movement, depended above all upon Hebburn for jobs, to some extent on Newcastle and South Shields, but only to an insignificant extent on Wallsend. Hebburn stood out as a major centre of net inflow of workers. Wallsend and Gateshead both received major flows from areas farther away from the river but both sent even higher proportions of their resident workers to Newcastle. The County Borough of Newcastle-upon-Tyne declined in population by 70 000 or almost one-quarter in the 1965 to 1971 period and has increased greatly as a focus of commuting movements. In 1966 over 50 per cent of the economically active residents of Gosforth Urban District and between 25 and 50 per cent of those in Whitley Bay, Longbenton, Castle Ward, Newburn, Wickham, and Ryton—authorities with over 190 000 inhabitants—travelled to work in Newcastle.

Fig. 8. Motorway plan for Newcastle upon Tyne, 1971

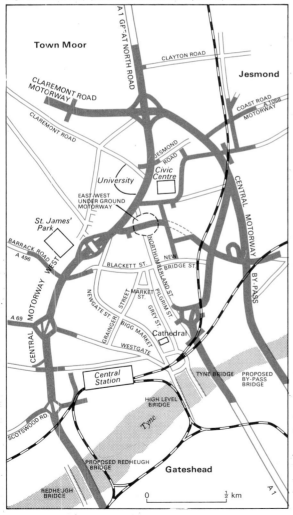

Altogether the net daily gain of workers by Newcastle was over 50 per cent.

In recent years extensive central area reconstruction has begun in Newcastle upon Tyne, and with approval of the new urban motorway plan by the Minister for the Environment in summer 1971 even more radical reconstruction lies ahead (Fig. 8). In the past the development of new bridging points has in turn built up new commercial growth foci—Grey Street, then Westgate, Grainger Street, and Newgate Street, and with the opening of the Tyne Bridge at the end of the 1920s, the rise to pre-eminence of Northumberland Street. New motorway traffic routes and associated urban renewal—including conversion of Northumberland Street into a pedestrian shopping street and the new Civic Centre and expansion of the University precinct to the north of the Haymarket—are creating yet another commercial core along Percy Street, until now a very run-down shopping area. Already in 1971 one of the leading department stores decided to move from Market Street to build new premises in Percy Street, and a new £26 million complex of 120 shops, adding well over one-quarter to the present floor area of shopping in central Newcastle, has been approved for the part of the street backing onto Eldon Square. New office employment is being provided on a large scale nearer to the river on Pilgrim Street and in the big new office precinct to be built around All Saints Church. With these major commercial and office developments there seems to be ample evidence that Newcastle will retain its pre-eminence as the 'administration office' for the North-East.

Teesside

The Teesside sub-region defined by the Northern Region Economic Planning Council (N.R.E.P.C.) has 580 000 people but this includes Hartlepool C.B. and, to the south, a number of Cleveland authorities already considered as part of the rural fringe. The economy of this sub-region is dominated by manufacturing employment—51·5 per cent of the whole employment in 1968 as compared with 37·7 per cent for the North-East as a whole, 38·6 per cent for Tyneside/Wearside and 44·9 per cent for Darlington. Teesside is 'an industrial Hercules' as a recent President of the Board of Trade put it, and there can be no doubt about the physical impressiveness of its industrial landscape: domes, fractioning columns, chimneys, blast-furnaces, rolling mills, and gantry cranes standing out starkly above the low estuarine plain (Fig. 9).

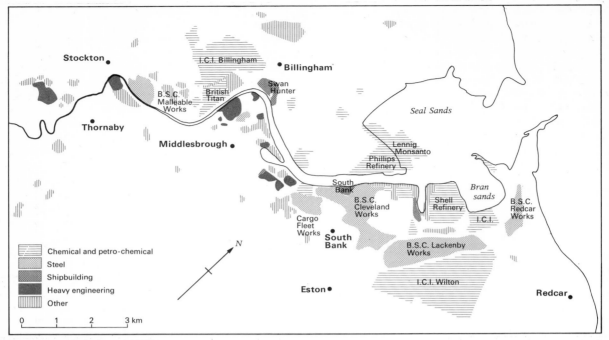

Fig. 9. Teesside industry, 1970

As it lies well away from the coalfield and with iron-ore mining in Cleveland dead, employment in extractive industry is naturally of little significance on Teesside. Construction jobs equal the regional average but service employment is well below it—38·0 per cent as compared with 45·2 per cent for Tyneside/Sunderland (and 53·2 per cent in its North Tyneside subdivision). For men the emphasis on manufacturing employment is even more marked—42·9 per cent of the total for 1968 on Tyneside/Wearside, 50·2 per cent in the Darlington sub-region, and 60·6 per cent on Teesside. More exactly, 19·6 per cent of all Teesside male employers were in metal manufacture, 17·3 per cent in chemicals, 9·7 per cent in engineering and electrical goods, and 3·2 per cent in shipbuilding and marine engineering.

Steel-making is located to a very small extent at Skinningrove, on a much bigger scale on the southern and south-western sides of Hartlepool, but above all on the south side of the estuary. New capacity at Lackenby is leading to closure of iron- and steel-making, but not of rolling mills at Skinningrove and Cargo Fleet. The probability of a very big new plant at Redcar suggests that by the end of the 1970s all iron- and steel-making on Teesside will be concentrated on the south bank.

Although there are other firms, including important new developments, Teesside chemical manufacture is dominated by I.C.I., employing just under 30 000, mainly in the two works at Wilton and Billingham, closely linked by pipeline connections under the Tees. Major new units, notably for the bulk production of ethylene and ammonia, have greatly increased output and, except for the possible diversion of some future expansion to the continent, expansion seems likely to continue. As in steel, however, the workforce is unlikely to increase. In part associated with the chemical trade is oil-refining at two units, one on either bank of the estuary, both built in the 1960s. A major role is played by structural engineering and also by firms producing heavy equipment and machinery and process plant. Structural engineering grew up to use the local steel; equipment and process engineering developed originally to meet steel plant needs but later diversified to build plant also for oil, chemical, and non-ferrous metal firms at home and overseas.

Apart from the plant and equipment makers, the basic trades of Teesside are heavily dependent on the estuary. In the ten years to 1970/1 the tonnage handled by the Tees and Hartlepool Port Authority went up from seven to twenty million tons. General cargo business has increased and the port operates container facilities, but bulk traffic dominates. In the past this was made up principally of iron ore, but now oil is far and away the chief cargo with iron ore second. Teesport, developed in the post-war years and in the main during the last decade, can now take 83 000 d.w.t. vessels, but still bigger developments are now occurring nearer the mouth of the estuary. By 1971 the 35-foot channel there was being deepened to 47 feet for three miles from the sea, so permitting entry of 150 000 d.w.t. vessels. On the south side of this channel a £6 million, ten million ton per year iron-ore dock will open at Redcar in 1972, and on the north bank dredging is being accompanied by the reclamation of the great area of Seal Sands, where major new industrial developments are occurring.

Economic growth on Teesside is impressive but deceptive. The sub-region above all turns out producers' goods, made in huge capital-intensive establishments with a relatively small labour input. Expansion involves more plant but may be accompanied by reduction in the number of jobs. Figures derived from the *Teesside Survey and Plan (Teesplan)* show that, whereas employment in chemicals increased by 11 000 (or almost half) between 1954 and 1966, employment in metals and in engineering and shipbuilding fell by 4100 and 3300 respectively. Looking ahead to 1991 *Teesplan* suggested a contraction in all these categories. If the major new Redcar steel plant is built, employment in metals will probably hold its own. Meanwhile population and numbers seeking work increase.

It is estimated that by 1991 companies already present on Teesside will provide about 260 000 jobs, but that some 300 000 will be needed to employ the projected population. In short, in the period to 1991 there must be a net increase of 1400 to 1700 new jobs each year. In the five years to 1971 the average job creation rate was 1500. If the target is reached, the change to more diverse manufacturing and to the service sector will be pronounced. Success is to a considerable extent dependent on government policy, through Development and Special Development Area policy, and through action in the nationalized industries—plans for steel obviously being critical for Teesside. The switch from investment grants to taxation allowances, and the granting of Special Development Area status for the whole of the coalfield, Wearside, and Tyneside in 1970/1, severely injured Teesside efforts to diversify, and in 1971 unemployment rates there rose especially rapidly. In March 1972 the government returned to the investment grant principle.

The urban fabric of Teesside grew up piecemeal. Middlesbrough with its rapid economic growth, and without the traditions of civic pride which maintained a metropolitan appearance in the core area of Newcastle, is the biggest of the communities built close to the ironworks. It is 'the very prototype of a town born and reared in the past century' and, as the first Medical Officer for Health put it, '. . . few worse sites in which to found a large and increasing town could have been found'.[1] In the last thirty-five years Billingham has emerged as a dynamic new community, very much better designed and more affluent than the older industrial townships like Grangetown or South Bank. Within the last decade new shopping centres have been built on the outskirts of the conurbation, particularly at Billingham and Thornaby, and after April 1968, when the new Teesside County Borough came into being, reconstruction began in the urban core of Middlesbrough, till then extraordinarily drab and ill serviced. Looking ahead to the last years of the century, *Teesplan* aims for a more integrated conurbation, with new communities emerging beyond the edge of the present built-up area.

Both the Royal Commission on Local Government (the Maud Report) and the government White Paper of 1971 provided for a very much extended Teesside region, stretching northwards into Durham, including Hartlepool and much of the North Riding. Local reaction to these proposals was surprising. 'The sheep-farmer of Danby or the fisherman of Whitby has little in common with the steelworker or commercial executive of Teeside or Hartlepool', wrote the *Teesside Journal of Commerce*, and problems faced in the various districts that would be taken in by the enormous Teesside proposed by the Royal Commission require far more local knowledge and understanding than would be provided by a local authority of the nature envisaged.'[2] To the pit-village dweller in turn, industrial Teesside is an alien world; the scathing tone of references to 'the great Teesside conurbation' in 'Close the Coal-house Door' will be recalled.

Hartlepool, created in 1967 from the formerly fiercely independent West Hartlepool C.B. and Hartlepool M.B. was excluded from Teesside. This was unfortunate, for in the 1960s, and particularly in the last few years, major developments have filled in some of the wide pasturelands which till then separated West Hartlepool and Seaton Carew from Haverton Hill and Billingham: the Greatham steelworks, the Phillips Imperial refinery, and more recently developments on Seal Sands. By 1966, 5–10 per cent of the economically active residents of West Hartlepool travelled to work in Billingham and 10–15 per cent into Stockton R.D., against negligible return flows.

Hartlepool has suffered severe blows to its traditional heavy industries. The closure of its steelworks threatened twenty years ago was avoided, but as activity has shifted to the new Greatham works, the North works has gradually been run down into a depressingly dead-looking, black, corrugated-iron eyesore with consequent loss of jobs. Even Greatham has suffered closure of some units of plant, so that by November 1971 there had been 1500 lost jobs or declared redundancies in Hartlepool steel-making since the beginning of the year. The Gray shipyard and the Hartlepool paper-mill have both closed during the 1960s and in the eight months to May 1971 almost a dozen engineering firms in the area laid off a total of 500 men. Population in Hartlepool C.B. grew by only 1·8 per cent between 1961 and 1971 as compared with 5·7 per cent for Teesside C.B. and in the three midsummer months of 1971 unemployment there averaged 8·2 per cent as compared with 6·4 per cent on Teesside—by November the unemployment rate for males was about 12 per cent.

The Darlington sub-region

Although it had iron-making capacity, nineteenth-century Darlington was above all concerned with wrought iron and iron finishing, and later with the use of steel in engineering and other metal-working trades. It retains some elements of the old specializations today. Albert Hill, the centre of the old iron trade, is still a drab part of the town. On the south side is the Cleveland Bridge and Engineering Works, descended from a former finished-iron enterprise. In the inter-war years engineering, with railway workshops prominent, was still of major importance, but already Darlington was more buoyant than Teesside. In 1932, in the trough of the depression, its monthly unemployment averaged 33·5 per cent, high in comparison with Newcastle's 26·7 per cent but favourable as compared with 41·9 per cent in Middlesbrough and 44·6 per cent in Gateshead. By 1937, a year of relative boom conditions, the

respective rates were 9·1 per cent, 14·3 per cent, 15·2 per cent, and 28·8 per cent. After the war the district became more diversified, notably with the development of the Aycliffe industrial estate. Textile employment was boosted by the arrival of Paton and Baldwin from the West Riding soon after the war. Since then this firm has built smaller subsidiary plants in South-west Durham. By 1967 Textiles (S.I.C. order X) employed 6·8 per cent of the workforce in the Darlington sub-region as compared with only 1·3 per cent in the North-East. With only 4·6 per cent of the regional labour-force, Darlington had 24·1 per cent of the employment in textiles. Engineering, however, remains pre-eminent (S.I.C. order VI), being 3 times as important as metal manufacture, the next order (V) in the percentage of total male employment in manufacturing. In 1963 Cummins began to build two Darlington motor industry plants, for diesel engines and components.

The opening of the Darlington by-pass, the earliest and southernmost part of the Durham motorway, emphasized the town's 'gateway' location for the North-East in relation to the rest of Britain. In 1967 the Darlington sub-region had 4·6 per cent of all employees in the region, 5·8 per cent of those in manufacturing, but its share of additional employment from I.D.C. approvals in the six years to the end of 1968 was 8·0 per cent. Unemployment rates have remained fairly low—3·7 per cent as the average for the three midsummer months of 1971 as compared with 6·4 per cent on Teesside. In its projections of population 1967–81, the *Outline Strategy for the North* suggested a 20·0 per cent increase for the Darlington sub-region as compared with 24·7 per cent for Teesside, 4·3 per cent for Tyneside/Wearside and 7·5 per cent for the North-East as a whole.

REFERENCES
1. M. LOCK, *Middlesbrough Survey and Plan* (Middlesbrough Corporation, 1946), pp. 9, 46.
2. *Teesside Journal of Commerce*, p. 172, August 1969.

6 Policy and the North-East: I. The Industrial Level of Decision-taking

The economic and social character of an area is moulded by a multitude of decisions which shape the landscape and are affected in turn by the physique of the area, its past human activity, and its position within the nation. International considerations now play an increasing part. In the past, decisions were taken individually; nowadays they are made by bigger organizations having a wider knowledge of conditions, but they are made at three critical levels, frequently still not co-ordinated—the level of the company or industry, the level of the local or regional planner, and finally the level of the national planner. Through its legislative guidelines, government greatly affects regional or local authority planning, through its regional policies and the nationalized industries it has great influence also on the decisions of companies (Fig. 10).

Coal and electricity policy

In spite of the closure of some pits, 140 000 men were still employed in the region's coalmines in 1958. In that year the rate of closure was accelerated, and in the autumn of 1965 a still more vigorous rationalization programme was embarked upon, following the White Paper on Fuel Policy. It was anticipated that this would close forty-eight collieries in the following three to four years with the loss of 30 per cent of the jobs in mining. It was still hoped that natural wastage would provide the necessary decline in the workforce. However in November 1967 another White Paper on Fuel Policy inaugurated a four-fuel policy giving less priority to coal and even more rapid contraction was expected. In the North-East the decline seemed likely to be catastrophic—immediately after the White Paper it was suggested that there might be a fall from 75 000 jobs in 1967 to 40 000 in 1971, 26 000 in 1975, and 6500 in 1980. So far decline has been slower than was forecast. Between November 1965 and July 1970 the number of pits in the region fell from 105 to 52, but a revival in demand for coal in 1970 caused the N.C.B. to try to recruit 3000 more miners in the region: by early 1972 about 44 000 still worked in the North-Eastern pits but further contraction seems inevitable. The problems of the coalmining industry are attributable, in part, to changes in government policies with regard to fuel; the situation of the electricity industry shows the effects of the lack of close liaison between nationalized industries, each striving to minimize its own costs.

At the end of the 1960s the North-East was remote from the main concentrations of British electricity generating capacity and from the main flows of power through the grid—it had almost an 'island' power economy with only tenuous links with the national core area.[1] The region has a number of small power stations, some decidedly market-orientated like the Skelton and North Tees plants on Teesside or the small Darlington station, others well located from the point of view of both coal supply and electricity demand as at Sunderland and on the Tyne. By national standards the only big station is at Blyth where two units have a capacity of 1523 MW and are located near the largest and lowest-cost mines in the Northumberland coalfield.

By the mid-1960s it was realized that economic growth, and particularly that in the Teesside sub-region, required new generating capacity. A site at Seaton Carew, south of Hartlepool, was chosen. Heated controversy about the type of plant to be built divided the C.E.G.B. and the N.C.B. Early in 1967 the C.E.G.B. asked for Ministry of Power approval to build a 1300 MW nuclear unit using the Advanced Gas-cooled Reactor (A.G.R.). The N.C.B. replied by questioning the economics of the whole nuclear power programme which it estimated had already lost it a market for fourteen million tons of coal and of the order of 28 000 jobs. The N.C.B. attack centred on the high construction costs of nuclear stations—though costs had been falling rapidly—and on the unreasonably high prices for coal which nuclear station propagandists were said to employ in their cost comparisons. In autumn 1967 the C.E.G.B. claimed £6 million would be saved annually by using nuclear power rather than coal, but the N.C.B. insisted that the £2·50 per ton of coal upon which this figure was based reflected average Durham costs—not those at low-cost pits from which it intended to supply Seaton Carew. Eventually, after a full cost-benefit analysis, the Minister gave permission for the nuclear station. National economic interests had triumphed over sectional interests, one North-Eastern sub-region over another. Many

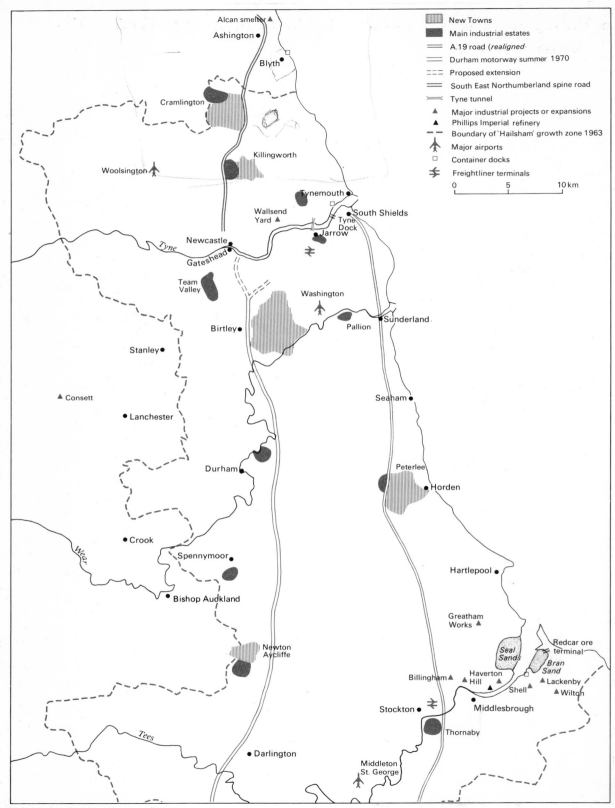

Fig. 10. Leading economic developments in the industrial North-East

hundreds of construction jobs and valuable calls on services are being provided in the Hartlepool area, pollution on Teesside will be less than in a thermal station, and nuclear engineering in the big electrical firms of Tyneside has received a much needed boost; but an estimated 7000 mining jobs have been put at hazard in County Durham. The *Teesside Journal of Commerce* concluded that the decision was right and that miners would have to reconcile themselves to commuting to the industrial areas. 'Manufacturers are unlikely to be attracted to small villages that were previously dependent on coal, but they will find advantages from being in a national growth zone like Teesside, with its excellent sea. rail, road, and air links.'[2] The logic of that statement cannot have been of much comfort to hundreds of families in the pit villages.

Disappointed at Seaton Carew, the N.C.B. was successful in inducing Alcan to design its proposed aluminium smelter at Invergordon in Aberdeenshire to use Northumberland coal and then, instead, to build the plant and a power station at Lynemouth. In this case too there was a clash between the interests of nationalized industries and sub-regional ambitions. The N.C.B. offered Alcan much lower rates than those it charged to the C.E.G.B. and to the British Steel Corporation. Teesside had offered aluminium companies an alternative and first-class site at Seal Sands.[3] In 1970 the N.C.B. argued that because coal mined at Ellington and Lynemouth had been diverted from export to the supply of the Alcan power station it should be permitted a large extension of open-cast coal-working in the North-East.

After contraction in the years following 1958, so as to protect the deep mines from the full effects of the reduced demand for coal, open-cast operations were again extended in the late 1960s because of their low costs—estimated on average in early 1971 as £4·50 a ton for open-pit coal as compared with £5·20 for shaft-mined coal. The North-East has some major open-cast operations. In one, at Widdrington just west of Druridge Bay, 600 men were employed in spring 1970 producing 25 000 tons weekly from an estimated 30 million ton outcrop, worked over 2000 acres. The impact on the environment along the A1068, and immediately behind the fine beach and sand-dune sweep of Druridge Bay, has been deplorable. In 1970, with the prospect of at least short-term coal shortages, the N.C.B. Opencast Executive applied for permission to open a major new site at Butterwell near Longhirst, Morpeth. At the Public Inquiry in August 1970 it was claimed that the operations would provide work for about 500 men for ten years and, through wages, add £750 000 annually to purchasing power, mainly in the locality. On the other hand a considerable acreage of Grade 3 agricultural land—good land, well farmed—and anything up to 50 acres of woodland and hedgerow would be lost. The project was strongly opposed by local interests, and the application was refused.

Developments in steel

Until after World War II, except for a few short periods, the North-East was the leading steel-producing district in the country. After the war, as steel demand shifted to lighter lines, South Wales achieved and later increased its lead. Within the region such intrinsically ill-favoured locations for iron- and steel-making as Skinningrove and West Hartlepool were kept alive. At the latter, business expanded because of the initiative of the South Durham company in entering the market for large-diameter gas and oil pipe. At Lackenby a big new steelworks and structural mill were built in the 1950s. By the late 1960s a new oxygen steelworks was building at Lackenby and the decision was then taken for a major ore dock at Redcar. Rationalization by the B.S.C. will lead to closure of iron and steel-making plant though not necessarily of rolling mill operations at outlying locations. The future of Consett provides an especially critical problem.

In 1966, when the Benson Report recommended use of iron-ore carriers of at least 65 000 d.w.t. and location of steel-works nearby, it was realized that Tyne Dock at Jarrow and the Consett Ironworks were at risk. It was at that time estimated that annually the Consett Iron Company spent £22 million on wages and on services in North-west Durham. Concurrently the management of this still independent concern was spending money on a large scale to extend capacity to two million tons of oxygen steel, a total far beyond the ability of the ironworks to support or the market to justify. The B.S.C. made arrangements to bring supplementary supplies of molten iron by specially designed rail vessel from Cargo Fleet. In 1972 Redcar ore dock will replace Jarrow as the import point for iron ore. Nearby coking coal supplies have been exhausted and supplies must come from East Durham. There is no local market for steel and the regional market is of declining significance.

By spring 1970 Consett works employed about 7600, including general service and haulage employees. Independent road hauliers, the British Oxygen Company, and tar and slag firms pro-

The launching of Tyneside's first super-tanker, May 1969, viewed from Hebburn. Tugs are needed to handle such a large vessel launched into a comparatively narrow river

vided 400 to 600 more related jobs. Taking into account the further effects through loss of local and sub-regional purchasing power, it was estimated that as many as 14 500 jobs in North-west Durham would be lost if the whole works closed. Much more probable is the closure of the iron-works or even, additionally, of the steel plant, so that the finishing mills would roll slabs brought from Teesside. Even so, the drift away of men if such a development occurred would reduce the female labour force too, and this fear deters new industry. There have been considerable new investments in the area, for instance the American firm Patchogue Plymouth, makers of woven polypropylene, a backing for carpets, chose Consett in 1968 as the site of its first European plant.

By 1970–2 Teesside was the subject of another major steel policy decision—should one of the B.S.C.'s planned ten million ton per year 'green-field' plants be located there? Undoubtedly the area possesses considerable attractions: big sites and deep water, with skilled metallurgical labour available as older works close. Pressure from Teesside is naturally in favour of such a develop-

ment and the B.S.C. itself has submitted plans for the works to the Teesside Council. Looked at from a national rather than regional point of view however, it is highly questionable whether the works should be located in this region rather than much nearer to major markets which have no steel plant of their own.

Shipbuilding

The post-1945 development of North-East ship-building is a story of disappointments—of under-capacity when orders were good, because of in-adequate material supplies, and, after yards had been modernized and supplies became abundant, low operating rates because of the keenness of international competition. In the first period delivery dates lengthened, so that competitors gained ground. The problem was also one of failure in national steel development and distri-bution policy: priority given to the expansion of light steel capacity left reconstruction of the heavier trades of Scotland and the North-East lagging behind.

In the late 1950s yards were modernized and

their methods improved. Swan Hunter and Wigham Richardson (now Swan Hunter) claimed that in the three or four years to 1960 labour costs per ton of steel used were cut from £35 to £25, but the rationalization was not sufficiently thorough-going. From 1956 Britain lost its lead in shipbuilding to Japan, and European competition became much keener. Lower prices began to attract abroad even the orders of British shipowners.

The 1962 report of the Patton committee on European competition suggested that their yards were only slightly better equipped or laid out, but that, combined with fewer unions and less job demarcation, there was a closer identification between workers and management. Steel throughput, the most vital index of operating efficiency, was higher than in British yards. In 1952 U.K. yards built 30 per cent of the world's tonnage, Germany 11·6 per cent and Japan 12·2 per cent: by 1963 their respective shares were 12·2, 11·6 and 25·1 per cent. Unemployment began to rise in North-East shipbuilding centres, and in 1962 William Gray of West Hartlepool was the first major British shipbuilder to fail in the post-war period.

In March 1966 the Geddes Report[4] recommended that shipbuilding firms should be merged into a few regional groups, each with four to six yards specializing in different types of ship, having about 8000 to 10 000 operatives and an annual production of some 4–500 000 tons a year. Its suggestion that the fifteen marine-engine works in Britain be reduced to three or four has not been followed, although Swan Hunter, the largest firm in the region, has given up engine construction. Geddes recommended that as steel makes up about 20 per cent of the cost of a merchant ship, steel price concessions should be given. On this point the steel firms demurred and, after 1967, the B.S.C. reduced discounts already given to shipbuilders and subsequently raised prices. The Geddes Report was followed by the Shipbuilding Act 1967 and establishment of a Shipbuilding Industry Board to provide grants and loans for the necessary reconstruction. By late 1971, under its guidance and prompting, twenty-two of the twenty-seven yards studied by Geddes had been merged into seven groups. One of these, Swan Hunter, controlled all the yards on the Tyne and Tees; two others, Doxford and Sunderland and Austin and Pickersgill, controlled the yards of the Wear. Over this period demand improved but costs rose rapidly thus narrowing profit margins or eliminating them altogether. Although it was possible to include cost-escalation clauses in contracts, these usually provided only for increases of about 5 per cent annually whereas in fact from 1968 to 1970 costs went up by 8–10 per cent a year. In orders booked in 1968 Doxford and Sunderland allowed for an annual 5 per cent wage rise, but, over the next two years, the increase averaged 16 per cent.

It became clear that the secret of success in Japan and in the best continental yards lay in physical and organizational developments which for various reasons British yards were ill-placed to introduce. The Arendal yard in Scandinavia pioneered the flow-line method of assembly, ideally a straight-line movement from the steel yards through the sub-assembly shop to the berth. Sub-assemblies, made under cover and welded into the largest possible units before moving to the berth, reduced construction times and weather hazards. New techniques were adopted in marking out and cutting metal, and the Japanese in particular introduced more efficient welding techniques using high tensile steels developed in co-operation with associated steel firms. They worked to designs that economized in steel and gave greater operating efficiency to the bigger vessels. Already by the mid-1960s the Japanese could build such vessels in half the time taken in European yards.

Although there are long-established links with the steel-makers, a large proportion of the shipbuilding steel used in the region comes from Scunthorpe—in 1965/6 almost one-third of the ship plate was from there. Except for Haverton Hill and South Bank the shipbuilders are located well away from the steelworks, and access difficulties rule out the delivery of big plates, so that assembly has to start with smaller units. Amalgamation on the Geddes plan can go on, but the consequences of an early start and, on the Tyne and Wear, physical limitations, mean that sites are congested and not suited to the ideal, straight flow-line assembly.

Wearside is unsuitable for giant vessels except in the yards at the river's mouth. Between 1962 and 1968 the number of shipbuilders there was reduced from six to two but the attempts of the Shipbuilding Industry Board to bring about a merger of these two have failed. However, building ways have been realigned, sub-assembly sheds built, and by concentrating on series production of specialized vessels success has been achieved. Austin and Pickersgill has had spectacular success with its 15 000 ton SD-14, designed to replace the Liberty ship, 1967–70 orders totalling seventy-one vessels worth over £100 million. For a time it was not easy to match sometimes excellent plant with the necessary throughput—there was difficulty in feeding enough steel into one of the advanced cutting machines—but standardization has improved steel handling efficiency to a British record, and by late 1971 keel-to-launching times had been cut to three and a half months. Doxford also build dry-cargo vessels and have an especially high reputation for marine engines, but their yards were closed by labour disputes for more than one-third of 1970, and physical conditions there are especially difficult.

Elsewhere in the North-East the range of product is wider and firms continue to compete for the biggest vessels. In 1966 Swan Hunter merged with Smith's Dock of South Shields and of the South Bank yard, Teesside. Early in 1968 Swan Hunter merged with Hawthorn Leslie, whose yard at Hebburn turned out specialist merchant vessels, with John Redhead of South Shields (cargo liner specialists), and with the Vickers' yard at Walker. It was subsequently revealed that, at this time, two or three of these yards were 'on the verge of bankruptcy and closing down'.[5] Rationalization has concentrated more activity in the Wallsend focus of the enterprise; here, for example, a sophisticated panel-making shop was opened in 1971 to boost steelwork production and supply all five Tyne yards of the group.

In 1969 Wallsend launched the first of a series of 250 000 d.w.t. tankers, but quickly ran into troubles. These included increased prices for steel and other materials, labour troubles (formerly less prominent on the Tyne than in other shipbuilding districts) and rising wages, but fixed-price contracts had been accepted because of the keenness of international competition. By the early 1970s, it was still an open question whether the Tyne could overcome its organizational and human problems associated with the psychology of craftsmen in an assembly-line age, and the similar difficulties of adjustment in management attitudes.

A significant theme in North-East shipbuilding in the 1960s was the problem of the outlying yards. Grays of West Hartlepool failed in 1962, and in 1966 closure was announced for the Blyth shipyard which employed 1200. Early in 1968 the decision to close the Haverton Hill yard was announced. This case is particularly instructive. Specializing in bulk carriers and tankers, Haverton Hill was very extensively modernized between 1962 and 1965, and expenditure continued at a high level after that. The results were impressive: from 1964 to 1968 the weekly output of the fabricating shop almost doubled and building time was cut by between one-third and one-half. Yet capacity was never fully employed: equipped to build vessels of up to 150 000 d.w.t. it never built anything bigger than 80 000 d.w.t. Wage increases and shortage of labour were additional problems, but lack of proximity to other yards with which services could be shared was a serious defect. Closure was expected to affect not only 3000 directly but, through the multiplier effect another 5000 or so. Swan Hunter declined to take over Haverton Hill in 1967 but in November 1968 it was induced to do so at a cost of only £500 000, along with £1 million invested by the previous owners in the Swan Hunter Group and a £1 million grant from the Shipbuilding Industry Board. Immediately Haverton Hill was provided with orders for 100–150 000 d.w.t. carriers.

The Tyneside group's new foothold on the Tees raises the major long-term issue of a location for North-East coast construction of super-carriers. So far Swan Hunter has made do with slipway construction at Wallsend, but a building dock is reckoned both safer and cheaper; and Tyneside's lack of such facilities is highlighted by the new £15 million modernization programme at Harland and Wolff in Belfast which has provided such a dock. It was believed that the group might use its rescue of the Furness enterprise to induce the government to provide the £7–10 million needed for a giant new dock and associated plant aligned transverse to the existing small slipways at the Walker Naval Yard. But such a dock is of limited value unless new cranage is also provided and this in turn makes a straight-line layout of stockyards, fabricating sheds, and building-dock essential. It is doubtful whether this ideal layout could ever be provided at Walker. New Swan Hunter interests on the Tees raise the possibility that the new dock might be there, where ideal sites could be obtained. So far, however, there is no indication that this will happen.

REFERENCES
1. See G. MANNERS, *Geography of Energy* (Hutchinson, London, 1971), p. 167.
See also E. S. BOOTH, *Power Supply for 1970* (C.E.G.B.).
2. *Teesside Journal of Commerce*, September 1968, p. 184.
3. For details of the development see K. WARREN, *Mineral Resources* (Penguin Books, 1973), Chapter 9: 'The New British Aluminium Industry'.
4. *Report of the Shipbuilding Inquiry Committee* (The Geddes Report), (H.M.S.O., 1966), Cmnd. 2937.
5. SIR JOHN HUNTER in the *Newcastle Journal*, 11 August 1971.

7 Policy and the North-East: II. National Policies for Problem Regions

Under the Special Areas (Development and Improvement) Act 1934, Tyneside, Haltwhistle, and most of County Durham, were recognized as problem regions. Teesside was excluded. The Commissioner for Special Areas was empowered to acquire and transfer land to organizations willing to undertake redevelopment. As no financial assistance was provided the effect was slight, and even in 1937 at the peak of the revival, unemployment in the North-East was 80–85 000 more than if it had been at the level of London and the South-East, an excess equal to about 11 per cent of the region's insured workers.[1] The Special Areas Amendment Act 1937 provided very small financial help, but by September of the following year government assistance to new industry in all the Special Areas had provided work for under 15 000 persons.[2]

One major advance of this period was the establishment of the first industrial estates. Even in the 1920s North-East interests pressed for government help to diversify the regional economy by building industrial areas modelled on the Trafford Park and Slough estates established by private enterprise in 1896 and 1920 respectively. In May 1936 the government incorporated North-Eastern Trading Estates Limited and within less than two years it was claimed that over 100 sites, eventually to employ 10 000, had been let to tenants in the 700-acre Team Valley estate west of Gateshead.[3] War checked the rate of progress and the 4000 workers at its outbreak were mostly women. Other, smaller estates were begun at Pallion and at St. Helen's Auckland.

Before the war was over, government commitment to a regional development policy had been affirmed. The White Paper on Employment Policy, 1944, accepted that maintenance of a high and stable employment level was a primary government responsibility and that balanced regional economic growth was essential to achieve it. The Distribution of Industry Act, 1945, repealed pre-war Special Areas legislation and renamed the problem regions Development Areas. This was an Act 'to provide for the development of certain areas; for controlling the provision of industrial premises with a view to securing the proper distribution of industry'. The meaning of the word 'proper' was never spelled out. The Act required firms to give the Board of Trade sixty days' notice of intention to build any new industrial premises exceeding 10 000 square feet floor area. Ministry of Works Building Licences, introduced in the war, were retained as a means of exercising this control until 1954. The Town and Country Planning Act, 1947, reduced the minimum size of plant or plant extension requiring approval to 5000 square feet, and obliged the firm to obtain an Industrial Development Certificate (I.D.C.) from the Board of Trade saying that the development was in accordance with 'the proper distribution of industry'. Power to acquire buildings as well as land, and to give grants to help in moving key workers, plant, and machinery was given to the Board of Trade in the Distribution of Industry Act, 1950. However by this time a combination of export and balance of payments crises and persistent shortages was leading to a reduction in emphasis on Development Areas. Over 50 per cent of all new factory floor space was in Development Areas between 1945 and 1947, in 1948 only 22 per cent, and in 1949 15 per cent. Change of government in 1951 reinforced the swing away from an active Development Area policy.

The North-East revived in the early post-war period. Its basic industries were prosperous and expanding. Nevertheless, unemployment levels remained high by national standards. In 1951 the national rate was 1·2 per cent, but that of the North-East 2·4 per cent—in 1955 1·1 per cent and 1·9 per cent respectively. Prosperity in the old trades was checking the diversification needed to reduce the differential, acting as a brake on a necessarily painful process of economic adjustment.

By 1958 the steady post-war expansion in the basic trades was ending, with the exception of that in chemicals. Unemployment in the region rose to 3·6 per cent in 1959. The Board of Trade began to tighten its I.D.C. policy to steer more industry to the Development Areas. The Distribution of Industry Act, 1958, and the Local Employment Act 1960, introduced valuable new elements, notably in making grants and loans for any new employment-creating activity, not just manufacturing. Unfortunately, however, it diverted attention to localities and pockets of unemployment—'Development Districts'—aiming to remove symptoms rather than dealing with the disease. Generally, the region was in bad economic shape at this time. In 1961 the average unemployment rate was 2·9 per cent as compared with 1·4 per cent nationally. Only 26 per cent of the County Durham workforce was female as compared with 38 per cent generally.

A new Local Employment Act in 1963 provided for building, plant, and machinery grants and accelerated depreciation. By this time, too, a regional perspective was re-emerging above the pre-occupation with local problems. The existence of a favoured section in East Durham, east of the A1 and extending from Tyneside to Teesside was recognized in the concept of a 'growth zone' embodied in the 1963 White Paper on the North-East. In autumn 1964 a new government quickly committed itself to the establishment of Regional Economic Planning Councils and Boards and a more active regional policy. It introduced Office Development Permits to control office employment in the South-East and Midlands. The Industrial Development Act of 1966 raised the plant and machinery grant to 20 per cent for the U.K. as a whole and 40 per cent for Development Areas—and for a time the respective rates were 25 per cent and 45 per cent. From 1965, while the 5000 square foot minimum level for I.D.C. permission was retained generally, the threshold was lowered in the more favoured parts of the country.

With accelerated pit closure late in 1967, the government introduced an important differential into the Development Areas, designating as Special Development Areas those parts of the coalfield especially hard hit. In the S.D.A.s, firms taking government-built factories could get them rent-free for up to five years, as opposed to low rentals in the Development Areas. Building grants, 25 per cent in the Development Areas, were 35 per cent in the S.D.A.s. Loans were made available to cover the rest of building costs and there were operational grants for as much as 10 per cent of total costs for the first three years. In the North-East, seventeen Employment Exchange areas were given S.D.A. status. The effect was again to distort patterns of economic growth; immediacy replaced long-term economic desirability. In the three years to autumn 1970 an estimated 80 per cent of new industry in the North-East was established in the S.D.A.s.

In 1966 the Selective Employment Tax was introduced as a national tax on employers for each worker, but with rebates paid to manufacturing industry. This in itself introduced a differential element, a boost to areas like the North-East with a higher than average employment in manufacturing. After April 1968 the impact was increased when the rebate was confined to manufacturing industry in Development Areas. However in the following year this source of income was diverted to provide the funds to finance the assistance programme for the new Intermediate Areas, a change which cost the North-East £7 million a year. The Regional Employment Premium introduced in September 1967 provided the industrialist with a per capita premium for each employee in the Development Areas, a premium ranging from 47½p weekly for girls to £1·50 for men. By 1970, R.E.P. payments were £100 million annually of which £28 million was paid to firms in the North-East. The aim was to counterbalance the emphasis on heavy, capital-intensive trades, which investment grants had reinforced, and so to boost employment and assist in the introduction of labour-intensive trades (Table 9). R.E.P., however, now provided a disincentive to the rationalization that was essential if some of the heavy industries were to survive in new, more highly competitive situations, as for instance with British entry to the E.E.C.

The new Conservative government in 1970 made major changes in Development Area policy. It decided that the benefits of the Regional Employment Premium did not justify its cost and that the payments should cease in September 1974. In November 1970 it was announced that building grants would go up from 25 to 35 per cent in the Development Areas and from 35 to 45 per cent in the S.D.A.s, but that the 40 per cent cash investment grants in plant and machinery—as opposed to 20 per cent elsewhere—would be replaced by depreciation allowances. Unemployment subsequently began to rise sharply, and considerable efforts were made to introduce a new growth momentum, this time with an emphasis on infrastructure investment—an extended road programme in June, an allocation of £100 million in July 1971 for infrastructure in the Development Areas, and, later, major expenditure on the nationalized industries. In February 1971 S.D.A. status was extended to cover the whole coalfield, the Tyneside/Wearside conurbations, and Hartlepool; assistance to S.D.A.s was increased. So far results have not been impressive, but areas excluded from S.D.A. status have suffered, notably in the case of Teesside, where the unemployment rate has risen much more quickly than that of the region as a whole and where there are fears that lack of S.D.A. provision will deter potential light industry. Replacement of investment grants by allowances for taxation

TABLE 9
Capital investment, jobs created, and investment per job in sample North-East developments, 1968–70

	Capital investment (£ million)	Expected workforce	Investment per worker
Monsanto, Seal Sands, Teesside	£10m	100	£100 000
C.E.G.B., Seaton Carew Nuclear Station, Teesside	£91m	450	£202 000
Alcan, Lynemouth	£50m	900 (direct)	£55 000
		1900 (including miners)	£26 000
Hilton Davies Chemicals, Dudley	£2·0m	200	£10 000
Glaxo Laboratories, Cambois	£5m	250	£20 000
Fasson (self-adhesives), Cramlington	£0·7m	100	£7 000
Fasson (self-adhesives), Cramlington (extensions)	£0·25m	40	£6 250
N.C.B., Butterwell Site (forecast)	£6m	500	£12 000

purposes has been the most critical change. The impact on the North-East chemical industry has been especially important.

Chemicals and investment

Whereas Chemicals and Allied Industries (S.I.C. Order IV) employed 5·2 per cent of the North-East's male workers in 1968, on North and South Tyneside the proportions were only 3·5 per cent and 3·9 per cent respectively, and in the Sunderland sub-region, 1·9 per cent. In the Teesside sub-region the figure was 17·3 per cent and in Teesside C.B. 20·7 per cent. Billingham works increased its turnover between 1945 and 1959 almost fivefold, and in this period over £100 million was invested in the new works at Wilton. Already Teesside was the biggest petrochemicals focus in Europe. Growth continued, so that by 1972 Wilton represented an investment of £300 million. Other major chemical firms have come into Teesside in recent years.[4]

Between 1954 and 1961, with I.C.I. sometimes investing at the rate of £1m a month at Wilton, employment in chemicals on Teesside went up from 23 700 to 35 000. Subsequently, though investment continued, employment fell away slightly and the *Teesside Survey and Plan* has estimated that from 1966 to 1991 it will decline by 1500. Some have argued that investment grants led to a misuse of funds and failed to get to the heart of the Development Area's problems.[5] On the other hand this ignored the strong competitive pressures in the basic industries—if chemical manufacture were not continually being rationalized, I.C.I. would become uncompetitive as compared with the big continental groups and

many more North-East jobs would be lost.[6] Although increasing prices—for materials, labour, and equipment—played a part and confused the issue, the ending of investment grants in autumn 1970 provided a partial check on the theories. Extension and rationalization continue on Teesside, but there have been significant redundancies in 1971, and a noticeable feature of the years from 1970 to 1972 has been the switch of more and more investment from the United Kingdom to the E.E.C. and to the United States. In March 1972 the government announced new Development Area measures which included a return to the investment grant principle. Hopefully in the course of the next few years this may check the drift of chemical investment away from the region.

REFERENCES
1. M. P. FOGARTY, *Prospects of the Industrial Areas of Great Britain* (Methuen, 1945), p. 167.
2. *Report of the Royal Commission on the Distribution of the Industrial Population* (The Barlow Report), (H.M.S.O., 1940), Cd. 6153, p. 146.
3. *The Times Trade and Engineering*, North-East Coast Section, p. xxxviii, October 1938.
4. P. W. B. SEMMENS, 'The Chemical Industry of Teesside and South Durham', *British Association, Durham, 1970.*
5. J. BRAY, *Decision in Government* (Victor Gollancz, 1970).
6. K. WARREN, 'Growth, Technical Change, and Planning Problems in Heavy Industry, with Special Reference to the Chemical Industry', in M. CHISHOLM and G. MANNERS (eds.), *Spatial Policy Problems of the British Economy* (Cambridge University Press, 1971), pp. 180–212.

Much of the physical shape of development at the sub-regional level is determined by local authority or regional planning. In the 1930s the stricken condition of South-west Durham and the choice of a location near the A1 for the first industrial estate provided major indications of a shift of both opportunity and development policy from the west to the centre and east. English Industrial Estates Corporation policy since then has reaffirmed this growth corridor emphasis. In both 1960 and 1970 Team Valley, Spennymoor, and Aycliffe estates alone had 37 per cent of all the workers on industrial estates in the North-East. These are regrouping points for labour from the older coalfield villages. Their significance is related to the highly controversial theme of the D-class villages (Fig. 11).

The Town and Country Planning Act of 1947 required planning authorities to draw up a development plan. The Durham County Development Plan in 1951 squarely faced the changing economic prospects of the various sub-regions and outlined a related programme of physical planning. It classified the 357 villages of the county into four groups. In 70 of them, the A-class villages, substantial growth was expected and further investment was justified. In the 143 villages of class B, capital was needed sufficient to cope with a static population, and 30 C-class villages were to receive the minimum investment to provide for a slowly declining population. The remaining 114 villages, one-third of the total, were expected to suffer considerable loss of population and, when existing houses were

Fig. 11. Elements in the settlement pattern of County Durham. 'D' class villages were defined by Durham County Council in 1970 as 'Settlements in which new capital investment will be limited to the social and other facilities needed for the life of the existing property'

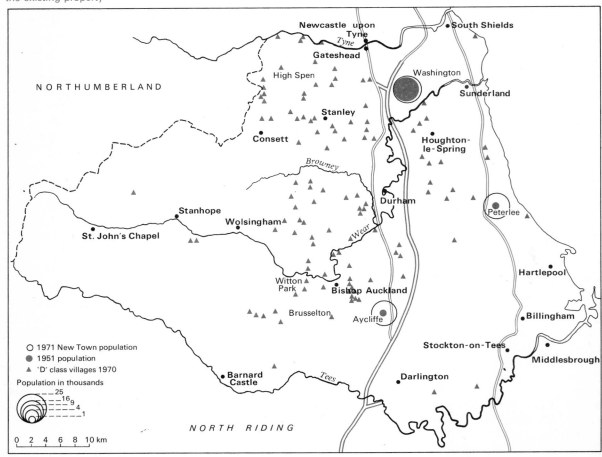

Dennis Wompra

Teesport. General cargo and containers can be seen in the foreground, in the middle left is slag from Cleveland steelworks. Across the river is the Phillips Imperial Refinery, and in the background Haverton Hill, Billingham, and Middlesbrough

vacated, they were to be replaced elsewhere. Over three-quarters of the D-class villages were west of the A1. Through the changing circumstances of the last twenty years, Durham County Council has held to this policy, though details have changed. Some very small villages have been wholly dismantled, others have all but gone. By December 1971, 35 of the 42 houses in Brusselton had been demolished, and in Witton Park, which became especially notorious because of frequent press and television coverage, the open spaces left by demolition were the physical signs of a decline which between 1950 and 1968 reduced its population from 5000 to 2000. Claiming that they have new viability, because of the spread of commuting, the D-villages continue the fight against extinction—eleven of them took their opposition to a public inquiry in Durham in November 1971.

In Northumberland there is no such comprehensive categorization of communities, but nonetheless there is a good deal of 'localism' and opposition to the county growth area programme. When, in 1968, Alcan chose Lynemouth for its smelter, a councillor at Bedlington, only six miles away, was reported as saying '. . . now that we have lost the smelter . . .', and when, a little later, a mid-Northumbrian industrial promotion body was suggested, there were inter-authority conflicts as well as general resentment of the county policy of concentrating new housing

and industrial development in its new towns of Killingworth and Cramlington.

At a higher level, and with less specific powers than the local authorities, the Northern Regional Economic Planning Council has also had to face up to the redrawing of the map of the North-East. In *Outline Strategy for the North*, March 1969, it moved away from the idea of the Tyne–Tees growth zone to delineate instead two 'economic growth areas'—a Tyne–Wear area with its base extending from south of Sunderland to Blyth and its apex at Hexham, and a smaller Teesside area (Fig. 12). These two areas and the rest of the eastern part of the region were to be linked by a major north–south growth corridor along the Durham motorway, and on to Morpeth by the Great North Road. Scarborough, Northallerton, Hexham, Morpeth, and Berwick were suggested as peripheral growth centres, and fifteen or so smaller market-towns were chosen as 'anchor points' for the rural areas. Conspicuously the whole of West Durham was left with no growth centre or anchor point a reaffirmation of the logic of Durham's D-village policy.

There are additional conflicts of interest between the major urban foci. Sunderland, feeling itself left out of development, has threatened to withdraw its contribution to the regional airport at Woolsington, north of Newcastle, and to develop instead Usworth airfield. Much more important has been the divergence of interest between Tyneside and Teesside. Some North-Eastern planners argue that priority in assisted economic growth should continue to go to the Tyne–Wear area, for this lacks the dynamic basic trades of Teesside and is moreover the economic and social core of the region, giving it character, epitomizing its personality and drive; indeed in one instance the sub-region was even categorized as 'the citadel of the North-East'. There is much to be said for this point of view, but on the other hand it can be argued that, as the only major metropolitan area of the region, Tyneside in particular has all the attractions of diversity and scale economies and should be able to survive and adjust automatically. Teesside with a much less balanced economy and poorer cultural and social facilities, needs help to make the breakthrough. The setting up of the Teesside Regional Organization for Industrial Development (T.R.O.I.D.), and early in 1971 Teesside's diversion of its contribution from the North-East Development Council to T.R.O.I.D. was an expression of the belief that after all it is Teesside which needs special provision. By mid-1972 however, T.R.O.I.D. was being contracted and N.E.D.C. was expanding its work on Teesside.

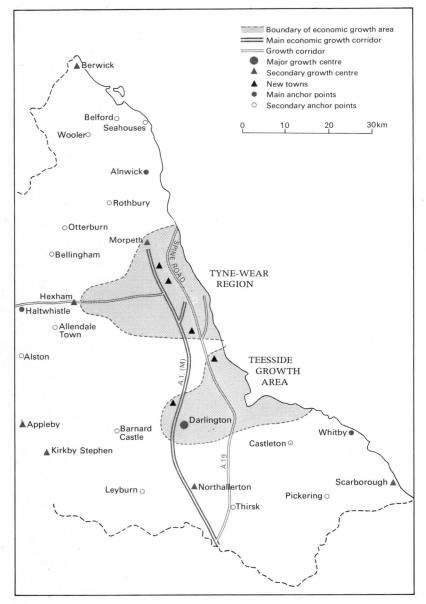

Fig. 12. Outline planning strategy for the North-East, 1969

9 The Shape of the Future North-East Region

Factors of production

The resource endowment of the North-East favoured economic growth in the nineteenth century: in the twentieth century, as demand and technology have changed, so regional material assets have declined. The lead- and iron-fields of the region are dead, and although there are new raw material supplies, such as potash and natural gas, they are relatively very much less significant than was coal. Gas is not only much more easily transported but policy decisions have made it available at comparable prices all over Britain. The region has abundant water resources but they are very unevenly distributed, so that Teesside, the only area with really extensive flat coastal sites and deep water, has the most marked deficiency in supply.

Abundant and skilled labour is a valuable regional asset but one which may waste or move away with time. In the case of the North-East both have happened. Skills appropriate to a nineteenth-century basic industrial structure require considerable adjustment to meet the needs of the late twentieth century. The basic educational facilities of the region are deficient,[1] and although now much improved, industrial retraining facilities were for long both inadequate and inconveniently located. After the trauma of prolonged unemployment, North-Eastern workers widely have a reputation for backwardness and intractability. In spite of recent strikes in the shipbuilding industry in particular there is no evidence that the region is worse than the rest of the nation in this respect, but it is the perceived rather than actual labour conditions that are decisive in attracting or repelling outside firms. In respect of labour rates the North-East generally has only a slight attraction to the cost-minimizing industrialist.

Much of the capital and enterprise for economic development was generated within the region in the nineteenth century. In the present century national concerns have taken over, with access to central sources of capital and frequently with their headquarters—and main office employment —elsewhere. The shipbuilding groups remain overwhelmingly regional, but the N.C.B., I.C.I., and more recently the B.S.C., have taken over from regional companies. The decision to locate the B.S.C. General Division headquarters in Glasgow—although Teesside has much more of its capacity—is a recent example of the way in which control may be removed from the region. In the middle of 1971, Power Gas of Stockton decided to move much of its operations and employment to a new headquarters in London.

Regional, national, and wider associations

The North-East suffers not only from the adjustments required of its old industrial economy, but also from its peripheral location in a national economy which is increasingly consumer-good and therefore mass-market oriented. In short its problems are perhaps not now primarily structural, but in the widest sense locational or spatial. In terms of centre–periphery relationships within Britain, the North-East is emphatically peripheral. South Wales, which had to make similar major structural adaptions, is much more accessible by motorway to the London–Birmingham economic core. Scotland, though still more remote than the North-East, is also in some ways more favoured, with a bigger national market protected by distance from the competition of core-area firms. Both Wales and Scotland have the advantages of national identity and therefore of political influence—a few years ago a North-East spokesman remarked ruefully that there was no Secretary of State for England. In short the North-East is less favoured in a number of ways than its main Development Area rivals.

North-Eastern regional growth in various categories of tertiary sector employment has differed from the national rate and those of other peripheral areas. In the sphere of public administration the region has more than kept up with national growth trends, though its spokesmen have urged much more devolution of government office employment. Relaxation of office controls since 1970 has not helped in the attraction of ordinary office employment, and the government has shown no readiness to consider the region's suggestion that cost bonuses should be paid to firms which move their offices away from London and the South-East. Insurance, banking, finance, and business, along with professional and scientific services, constitute a major employment growth sector, but although overall the North-East has exhibited growth in these categories, it still lags

TABLE 10
Estimated total number of employees, 1959 and 1970, selected British regions.

| Region | Thousands | | Percentage change |
	1959	1970	1959–70
Northern	1 298	1 270	−2·2%
Wales	951	935	−1·7%
Scotland	2 145	2 077	−3·2%
North-West	2 961	2 842	−4·1%
South-East and East Anglia	7 806	8 335	+6·7%
West Midlands	2 145	2 259	+5·3%
Great Britain	21 870	22 404	+2·4%

TABLE 11
Employment in the Tertiary Sector, 1959 and 1970, selected British regions.

| | As a percentage of total employment | | | | | |
| | Insurance, Banking, etc., and Professional and Scientific Services | | Miscellaneous Services | | Public Administration | |
	1959	1970	1959	1970	1959	1970
Great Britain	11·2	16·8	9·1	8·1	5·7	6·2
Northern Region	8·9	14·5	7·9	8·1	5·7	6·3
Scotland	11·4	16·6	8·1	8·0	5·3	5·8
Wales	10·7	15·1	7·9	7·5	6·5	6·9

well behind Scotland and Wales. Conversely, whereas the category 'miscellaneous services' has nationally been shrinking, it grew in the North-East.

These characteristics suggest that the region has by no means solved its structural problems, but clearly structural and locational problems are closely related. Position within Britain is an increasingly important factor determining the way in which, and the rapidity with which structure changes.

In the mid-1960s a reservoir of under-used labour was a major attraction of the Development Areas when a tight labour market, shortage and high prices for housing, and physical congestion —the characteristics known as 'overheating'— were major problems of the growth regions. By 1970–2, with rationalization spreading widely through British industry at a time of general recession, unemployment was rising even in such a former boom area as the West Midlands. This removed one of the obvious attractions of the Development Areas, and the decision to replace the investment grants and to remove Regional Employment Premiums by 1974 reduced their attractiveness on the capital and labour account still more. By this time too, Intermediate Area incentives—the introduction of which the North-East had vigorously opposed—may have been diverting growth to the 'grey' areas. It was already clear that the Regional Economic Planning Councils were much less powerful than had been hoped in the early days. As the former chairman of the Northern Economic Planning Council commented '. . . I was left in charge of a council of very competent people who had not the power to act and increasingly had less power of influence'.[2] With regionalism challenged and apparently in decline it gradually became clear that the North-East's problems must be looked at in a wider than merely national context.

As Britain moves into the European Common Market the regional impact is a matter of considerable speculation. The increased competition out of which favourable economic growth trends may emerge will undoubtedly centre on the east coast of Britain. Nevertheless, if British industry does prove on balance able to increase its penetration of the European market, the benefit will be especially marked in the South-East, especially if a Channel Tunnel is built. The North-East, peripheral in the United Kingdom economy, will be more peripheral still within an expanded Common Market. Sub-regional and local effects will depend on industrial structure and the competitiveness of the particular industry and firm. Coal demand from North Sea tidewater power stations may give a fillip to long-life coastal pits in the region; growing chemical activity may perhaps enable I.C.I. to increase still more the production of basic 'building block' chemicals on Teesside. North-Eastern steel communities will probably suffer, and Consett may find its position indefensible.

Much of course depends on policy decisions. To date most E.E.C. countries have followed national development area policies, but the Community is now evolving its own regional programme. A vital consideration will be whether the North-East is designated part of the 'peripheral zone' or merely part of the outer fringe of the 'central zone', for which no special help will be available. As the E.E.C. countries have no fringe of old industrial areas like those of Britain, but have instead extensive peripheral areas of largely rural economy such as Southern Italy, Aquitaine, Brittany, and—to a much smaller extent—Bavaria, it may well be feared that the problems of the North-East, Wales, or Scotland will receive less understanding and sympathetic attention.

The future North-East

Even though the pace with which adjustment of the North-East's economy will occur is in doubt, its direction is clear and the lineaments of the North-East of A.D. 1990 or 2000 can already be vaguely discerned.

By that time the dereliction which so badly marks the industrial core of the region and deters a good deal of potential economic growth will have been cleared. Employment and residence in the more remote, less physically favoured parts of the coalfield will have declined. Coal production will be confined to at most about ten pits within three to four miles of the coast. There will be continued relative decline in the status of Wearside, but contraction in the Hartlepool area may be reversed as deep-water facilities are provided on Seal Sands and the area separating it from the built-up parts of Teesside is developed. More of the region's commercial growth will be focussed in the two conurbation cores of Newcastle and Middlesbrough. Tyneside will exercise a strong locational attraction for consumer goods; Teesside's manufacturing economy will diversify and will increase in regional significance. Searching for open, pollution-free sites near to supplies of labour, much of Teesside's lighter industry will then be located to the west of the present built-

Dennis Wompra

Steel-making on north Teesside. In the background are the old Hartlepool works, which were formerly served by the small ore dock which lies in the Hartlepool dock system beyond. In the foreground are the Greatham steel-works, built 1958–62

up area, and by A.D. 2000 the land between Teesside and Darlington will be dotted with industrial estates and will be suburbanized. Darlington, at the junction of routes to Teesside, to Tyneside, and to the rest of Britain, will continue to grow rapidly; and northwards, Newton Aycliffe and Washington and the industrial estates at Spennymoor, Dragonville, Birtley, and Team Valley mark the first stages in the development of the linear city which some planners proposed in the early 1960s (Fig. 13). This emerging axial line of land-based growth already extends to the north of Tyneside in Killingworth and Cramlington new towns.

As affluence and mobility increase and the socio-economic structure of the region conforms more closely to the national average, population will spill out into the rural areas. Teesside workers will live in the narrow rural fringe which separates it from the coalfield and move more widely into Cleveland and the Vale of York. Darlington's commuters will spread up Teesdale and those from the new A1 and Durham Motorway growth foci will help to revitalize some of the villages in the lower parts of the dales of West Durham. Tyneside has already pressed far into Castle Ward and up the Tyne to Hexham. Housing incursions into the rural fringe will be matched by new calls on it for water, for space, and for recreation.

To the end of the century or even beyond, the North-East will probably remain a problem region. Special assistance will be needed to keep its standards of living near to the national average. Planning for economic decline over large areas will be needed but other localities will undergo substantial, even spectacular growth, and the region as a whole will still offer an increasingly valuable asset—space, the freedom from the quite uncontrollable swarming of people in the economically more favoured regions of Britain.

Few parts of Britain have urban views as impressive as the industrial spread of Teesside viewed from Eston monument, Durham Cathedral seen from the station on a moonlit night, or the City of Newcastle from the Tyne bridges. Few can match the North-East for rural splendour —the craggy wildness of the Roman Wall country west of the North Tyne, the haunting beauty and the clear strong air of the coast from Craster to the romantic ruin of Dunstanburgh Castle, the sombre forests of Kielder or Wark, and the charm of Coquetdale between the sandstone edges of Simonside and the woods and rhododendrons of Cragside. While these remain, even a problem region provides its ample compensations.

REFERENCES
1. *Report on Education*, Northern Economic Planning Council, 1970.
2. DAN SMITH quoted *Newcastle Journal*, 14 July 1971.

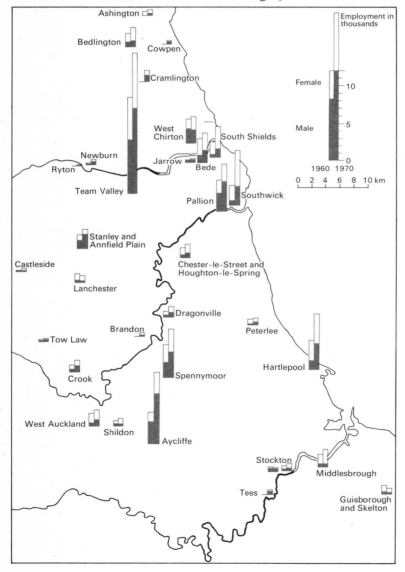

Fig. 13. Employment on North-Eastern industrial estates, 1960 and 1970

Further Work

For the student wishing to pursue his studies of the North-East there is a wealth of published information. Reference has already been made to some of these publications at the end of the preceding chapters. A valuable general text is *North England* by A. E. SMAILES (Nelson, 1968) which also contains a useful bibliography and has a good many excellent photographs. For an account of industry in the region the reader is advised to look at *Industrial Britain: The North-East* by J. W. HOUSE (David and Charles, 1969).

A number of publications provide an introduction to planning in the North-East. Some idea of the projects which have been attempted over the course of the last ten years can be obtained from:

The North-East: A Programme for Regional Development and Growth (Cmnd. 2206 H.M.S.O., 1963).

Challenge of the Changing North (Northern Economic Planning Council, 1966).

Strategy for the North (Northern Economic Planning Council 1969).

Teesside Survey and Plan, Volume 1 Policies and Proposals (H.M.S.O., 1969).

Other references which might be found useful include:

G. H. J. DAYSH and J. S. SYMONDS: *West Durham: A Study of a Problem Area in North-Eastern England* (Blackwell, 1951).

J. C. DEWDNEY (ed.): *Durham County and City with Teesside* (British Association, 1970).

D. DOUGAN: *A History of North-East Shipbuilding* (Allen and Unwin, 1968).

J. W. HOUSE and B. FULLERTON: *Teesside at Mid-Century: An Industrial and Economic Survey* (Macmillan, 1960).

K. WARREN: 'The shaping of the Teesside industrial region', *Advancement of Science*, 25, 1968, pp. 185–99.

G. MANNERS (ed.): *Regional Development in Britain* (John Wiley, 1972).

In recent years many important studies of particular parts of the North-East or of specific problems have appeared in the Research Series published by the Departments of Geography in the Universities of both Durham and Newcastle. Essays on North-Eastern subjects are also to be found in *Northern Geographical Essays in Honour of G. H. J. Daysh*, ed. J. W. HOUSE (Department of Geography, Newcastle University, 1966).

The North-East provides ample opportunity for studying the impact of New Towns on a region and the student is referred to the plans published by the Development Corporations of Aycliffe, Peterlee, and Washington New Towns, and those by Northumberland County Council for Killingworth, and Cramlington.

For map work there are the sheets at various scales published by the Ordnance Survey and also one-inch to one mile maps of the Geological Survey. More general information can be obtained from the *Atlas of Britain* (Oxford University Press, 1963) and from the Reader's Digest *Complete Atlas of the British Isles*.

Index